BARSAS GÅRDEN

Hanna Humberd

Copyright ©2016 by Hanna Humberd
www.hannahumberd.com

Originally Published in the United States of America by One In The Son Publishing Company.

All rights reserved.
No portion of this work may be reproduced or used in any manner without the written permission from the author, except in the use of brief quotations for review purposes.

Printed in the United States of America in 2016.
Original Cover Artwork by:
Gio Grönvall, Lovisa, Finland, 1960.
Cover Design by Joanna Humberd
Illustrations by Hanna Humberd

ISBN: 978-0-9973723-1-1

The Barsas Family

Back row: Grandpa Ivar and Grandma Klara, Mama Herdis and Papa Henning.

Front Row: older brother Ingmar, older sister Margareta, little sister Hagar and little brother Herbert in Mama's arms.

Map of Finland

Barsas Gården Blueprint

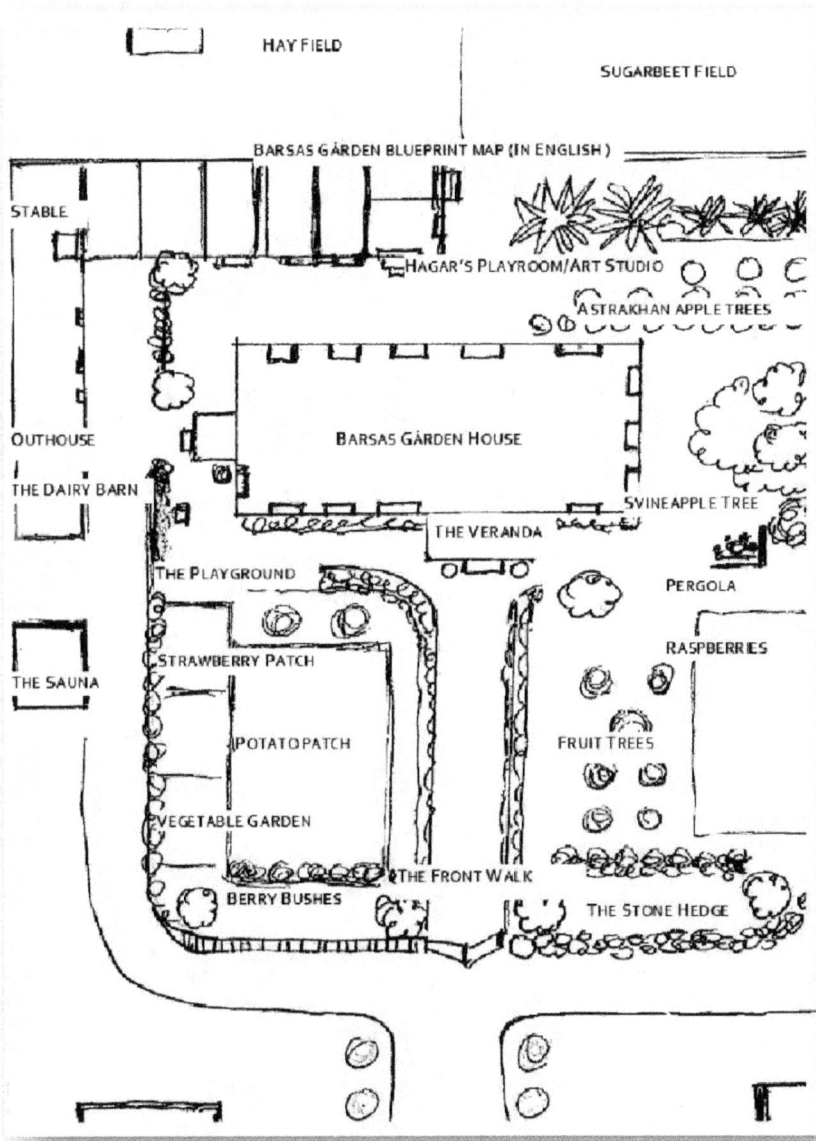

Cover artwork from a painting of Barsas Gården by Gio Grönvall, Lovisa, 1960.

Photographs by Ragnhild Frisk, Lovisa, 1950.

Photograph Restoration by Somil Kumar

Barsas Gården Illustrations

by Hanna Humberd

Dedicated to my Family in America

To James, my wonderful husband of forty-one years, to Joanna, my daughter, who has worked tirelessly to produce this book, to Peter, my older son, who is proud of his Finnish heritage and to Johnny, my younger son, who loves his mother. To all of them, and not one of them, knowing a word of Swedish.

Mama Herdis, Herbert, Ingmar, Hagar, Margareta and Kitty

Pronunciation Guide

Vowels:

a aw in father

e e in west (short) ay in café (long)

i i in Indian (short) ee in keep (long)

o oo in tool, o in not (short) o-as in fore (long)

u oo in rude

å o in yonder (short) o in fore (long)

ä a in apple (short) ai in fair (long)

ö *e* in *her* (short) *e* in *pew* (long)
  u in *fur* (before **a** long vowel)

Special Consonants:

c k in café (before hard vowel: a, o, u, å)
  c in city (before soft vowel: e, I, y, ä, ö)

j *y* in *yes*

k k in keep (before a hard vowel),
  ch in church (before a short vowel)

r (roll the r as in words with Spanish pronunciation)

Table of Contents

- 1 • Barsas Gården — 1
- 2 • Little Hagar — 9
- 3 • Sisters & Brothers — 19
- 4 • The Barsas Family — 31
- 5 • The Dairy Buildings — 39
- 6 • Memories of Deaths in the Family — 49
- 7 • Midsommar — 63
- 8 • Visits Within the Archipelago — 83
- 9 • Summer Fun — 95
- 10 • Elementary School — 103
- 11 • In the Attic — 113
- 12 • Christmas — 125

Herbert's Christening Day, 1950

Back Row: Grandpa Ivar Barsas, Holger Åström, Aunt Signe Barsas, Felix Fronden, Reverend Uncle Anders Gustav Stjernberg, Papa Henning Barsas holding little Hagar

Middle Row: Ingegärd, Aunt Eva Barsas, Aunt Ester Johanson, Aunt Birgit Viklund, Olga Fronden

Front Row: Grandma Klara Barsas, Margareta Barsas, Cousin Åke Viklund, Cousin Gunvor Viklund. Mama Herdis Barsas holding baby Herber with Ingmar Barsas on the far right

•1• BARSAS GÅRDEN

The name brings back happy memories of my childhood, of Mama and Papa, my siblings and all of my relatives.

We were four children in our family. There was my older brother, Ingmar, my older sister, Margareta, then me, Hagar, and my younger brother, Herbert. I always thought we were such a large family, especially when we had to travel by bus or taxi.

My childhood years were happy and harmonious. Mama and Papa had such pleasant personalities. Mama told us that she and Papa never had any fights. Although they had different opinions about this and that, we children never heard a harsh word between them.

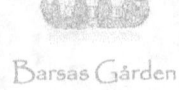

Barsas Gården

They worked so hard for us on the farm and Papa seemed to know a good joke for every occasion.

Our home was on a medium-sized farmstead in the country of Finland in a village called Räfsby (Refs-bee) 3.6 miles from the city of Lovisa.

Barsas Gården was an oasis. Everything was peaceful and calm. The atmosphere breathed charm and order. Lush, green lawns beckoned you to play on them. Wind energized you as it rustled through the treetops. Vivid colors bloomed. Scented flowers whispered.

Berries tempted you to pluck them and Astrakhan apples bubbled in the sun. The yards, so well-planned, reminded one of a landscaped estate.

The farmstead was a Wonderland. There were hay lofts to climb, barn nooks to search, kittens to discover, animals to pet and care for, wood to chop, a stone hedge to jump from, gates to swing on and hay stacks to slide down. For a child, it was an ever-changing playground to master and explore.

The property was encircled with a white picket fence to the west, and a thick, stone hedge to the east. To enter, you crunched up a sandy path and pushed through the two swinging, white gates guarded by two, huge, birch trees.

Barsas Gården

Red and black currant bushes greeted your arrival. To your left grew a vegetable garden, a potato plot and a strawberry patch. To your right, raspberry bushes and fruit trees posed with their bounty.

Rose-colored phlox and silver grass created a candy cane border up the path next to matching green lawns, while pink and yellow roses arched above them like so many ladies-in-waiting. We children had to painstakingly rake this sand path into beautiful, straight lines.

Finally, the path reached the front steps of the glass veranda where Mama had planted velvety, dark red roses. There, like a jewel in the midst of creation, sat our sunny, yellow, Barsas Gården home.

OUR MINI ORCHARD

I was so happy when our fruit trees bloomed. They looked like huge brides in romantic, white dresses.

Our bite-size front orchard featured a pear tree, a svineapple tree, a few apples trees, black, red and white currant bushes and raspberry bushes.

Sometimes when Aunt Elna Almen came over we girls picked big bushels of juicy berries. Mama then steamed them into juice with the Mehu Maija (meh-who my-uh) steamer.

Mama liked pears. Unfortunately, she never got a chance to eat a ripe one, for we children liked pears also and picked them long before they ripened. The svineapple tree was a big and beautiful tree but the apples tasted foul. Only the pigs (swine) liked them.

The raspberry bushes grew so tall you could get all tangled up in them.

THE PERGOLA

In front of the mini orchard, an outdoor seating area of sturdy, white wooden furniture fashioned a lush spot. Mama had planted aromatic caprifolia along a pergola, which is a white trellis set at an angle.

The Pergola was frequently used for cake and coffee parties in the summer. It was the perfect place to read an interesting book, enjoy a peaceful moment or chat with a close friend.

Under a birch tree, bloomed white rose bushes with a carpet of blue, forget-me-nots beneath it. I often picked flowers here for Mama, Grandma Klara and Aunt Eva to cheer them up, especially when they felt ill.

The back of our house was fenced in by yet another huge birch tree and white and lavender lilac bushes. From the second floor, we had a great view of our neighbor's fields.

Barsas Gården

We could also see the highway that led to Lovisa. If you followed that road in one direction, it led you to the city square, passed the impressive Lutheran church. In the other direction, the road led to the waiting waters of red, Valkom Harbor. The bus stop near Barsas Garden was called 'The Triangle'.

The Pergola

ASTRAKHAN APPLES

Outside our back window was an apple orchard. These were not just any old ordinary apples, however. From this orchard came the delectable, entrancing, Astrakhan apples. They were believed to have come from Russia.

The apples were pink and yellow. The exception was, when they were fully ripe, they became transparent. You could see bubbles of juice moving around inside the apple. The flavor was indescribable.

OUR HOMEMADE PLAYGROUND

Papa made us a playground by the kitchen entrance. Two iron chains hung down from a log, frame structure. Attached to these was a wooden board making a swing.

He built us a wooden sandbox with plenty of room for the boys to make mud roads with their cars beside girls making mud pies.

Papa also made us a bowling ball and a set of wooden pins which we loved to knock down. He really wanted to be a carpenter but because he had to take over the family farm when he became an adult, he had to work in agriculture. He still got in some wood-working whenever a chance came along.

Barsas Gården

THE GLASS PATIO

The glass patio at the main entrance was a popular place. It was called 'The Veranda.' The Veranda was an enclosed porch with huge windows creating a most pleasant atmosphere. Wild vines covered the windows, letting only soft light seep in through its multiple panes.

Underneath its stately windows sat long, white wooden benches. Inside on the left, was a sturdy, wooden, white table, and on the right hand side Mama had a clothespress where she pressed the wrinkles out of our clothes.

On rainy days, we played there with our dolls and cars. During parties in our home, the men liked to congregate on The Veranda, smoke pipes and talk about their farms.

YOUNG GARDENERS

In early spring, we began to clean up the garden. We children weeded the flowerbeds, raked the sand pathways, helped plant flowers for the new season and carried heavy buckets of debris to the compost pile.

By the kitchen, we helped create a patch of straight, blue delphiniums and star-shaped phlox in white, pink, red, lavender and dark purple. I loved the sheer, white baby's breath there that I added to my flower arrangements.

Alongside the stone hedge, we planted lovely, tall, yellow, butterball flowers.

Near the walk, Mama planted yellow daisies, called 'The Margareta Flower,' in between pink peonies and red peonies. The yellow and orange calendulas always reminded me of Mama.

The fragrance of pink peonies, red roses and multi-colored phlox still remind me of childhood summers.

My Grandpa Ivar hired a farm landscaper to plan the layout of the yards when he first built the farm in 1905. However, it is thanks to Mama and her agricultural know-how that we had such bountiful, beautiful gardens.

•2• LITTLE HAGAR

HAGAR IN NATURE

In the spring, when the snow was still on the ground, I picked big bundles of birch branches from the trees in front of our house. In my love for all things growing, I brought them inside. The warmth in the house, helped the little green leaves burst forth on the branches to everyone's joy.

We children liked to look for small, light blue, egg shells from the starlet birds. Sometimes they would build their nests in the birch trees. When the eggs hatched, the tiny shells dropped to the ground. We would find them under the trees.

Papa also showed me the best place to pick pussy willow branches. Enthusiastically, I waded through a slushy, country lane, between some farm fields and over a wooden bridge to the willow grove by a brook called Marbäcken.

I plunged my hands into the icy, cold water to pick branches with pretty white pussy willows for everyone to enjoy at home. The guardian angels must have been watching over me as I never fell into the chilly river.

It was sheer happiness for me to find these treasures in nature. In early spring, I also dug up buds of tussilaagon (too-see-lah-gun) buried deep in the clay because I couldn't wait for them to bloom. They opened up like little, yellow sunshines when taken inside.

HAGAR AND HER FAMILY

The stone hedge continued around our house with a hedge of fir trees in front of it. In early spring, I used to play house under the wide, fir tree branches.

I pretended that I was a Mama with children. I built a cozy nest using old, carpet scraps, boxes and little pots and pans. There was also a farm under those fir branches with an assortment of horses, cows, pigs, sheep and chickens, all made of pinecones, rocks and twigs.

In Finland, children were often outdoors from morning until evening, even in the wintertime. As infants, we were all bundled up and placed in a baby buggy to take our daily nap.

Fresh air was the best thing for good health, people believed. Sometimes babies slept for hours outdoors and woke up to the sound of birds twittering in the trees above them.

HAGAR THE LITTLE SHOPPER GIRL

I liked very much to go shopping to our two village markets in Köpbacka (Cher-bawcka). It took me almost an hour to walk there with my big shopping bag. I also carried a shopping list and a little cash purse.

After the sales lady was done filling my order, I half-dragged, half-carried the large bag home. Often, the grocery list involved polish sausage, margarine, yeast,

chocolate graham cookies and maybe a sucker or two--for me.

HAGAR'S FAVORITE SWEETS

My favorite sweets were suckers because they lasted a long time. The suckers with a blue and silver diagonal stripe were chewy caramel. The sucker with a red and silver diagonal stripe were chewy chocolate—like a tootsie roll.

All of us children liked Dacapo. It was regular chocolate but with an arrac (rum) flavor. There were Fazer's licorice bars and Jenki chewing gum and different flavored creampuffs dipped in chocolate.

In the summertime, we sometimes got ice cream from Valio's ice cream stand in town. There were only three flavors: vanilla, strawberry or chocolate and they came in wafer cones. The chocolate-dipped, vanilla ice cream on a stick was wonderful too.

THE PLAYROOM

I liked to play with dolls. Papa helped me make a playhouse out of the former servant's quarter. There was one little window with a lilac bush almost covering it from the outside.

The room had electricity and I was even allowed to spend the night there, but it was a little scary. I kept thinking I heard strange sounds in the night. Maybe it was just a mouse?

We thoroughly cleaned the room, since mice had occupied it for a long time already. Papa tore down an enclosed, wooden fireplace that was too old and unsafe to keep.

We dragged a bed, a table, an old armchair and a small cupboard down from the attic to make the room a real home. I made my little doll household even more pleasant by bringing in fruit from the orchard and flowers from the garden to brighten it up.

PUNISHMENTS

I didn't get in trouble much, but when I did I was given a spanking. Once I threw an apple at my little brother and it hit him hard in the head. Another time I pushed my sister. She fell in a ditch full of stinging nettles. Neither time had I pre-meditated to hurt them. I was just playing foolishly.

No matter how much I pleaded or begged for mercy, Papa still gave me some awfully hard spankings. Not even after I was spanked for saying, *sablar* (sah-bl-are), a Finnish swear word, did it dawn on me that I could have just said, "I'm sorry, please forgive me."

These three times, I was severely spanked by Papa. I hollered like a stuck pig in fright and shame. The more I screamed, the angrier Papa got. The angrier Papa got, the harder the spankings became.

Sometimes I was disobedient or nagged Mama, so that Mama had had enough. Mama gave me *luggisar* (luh-g-i-sar). She pulled the fine hair in front of my forehead or by my ears. It pinched so badly. The humiliation was the worst though. I was a sensitive child. For the most part I wanted to avoid any form of punishment.

GETTING A SHOT

Once I had a difficult case of bronchitis. The doctor had to come to our farm to give me a shot of penicillin. Papa had to hold me while the doctor jammed, a seemingly ten-inch needle, into my leg.

I kicked around and hollered in panic. My leg was stiff and sore for weeks. This was so much the case, I had to be carried everywhere, even to the bathroom. It explains why, in my younger family photographs, I always looked suspicious. I was sure the photographer was really a doctor, coming to give me a shot.

Once we had a nurse come to our home to give us children our yearly check-up. Mama said the nurse would also give us ultra-violet sunrays with a lamp. She proceeded to give us a Chalmette vaccination as well. The needle broke when she injected my sister! I still dread needles to this day.

The nurse also recommended some vitamins. Mama bought some but it looked like white chocolate to us. We children found them in a cupboard and promptly devoured the whole month's supply in one moment.

LABOR IN THE FIELDS:
My First Job for Money

The first job I was paid for was to thin out small, sugar beet plants in our sugar beet patch. Our sugar beet field started at the back stone hedge and rolled downhill to the river Marbäcken (Mar-bawk-en).

It was a chore to crawl up and down the hillside, row after row, on our knees, in the dirt. With a little hoe, we swiped away seven inches of little plants to make room for one plant to grow to a full sugar beet with a seven-inch circumference.

Our bodies ached in the evening. We counted the hours and days and weeks, figuring out how much we would

earn when the job was done. Many neighbors, mainly school children in Räfsby village, came out to help.

We competed on who could do their lines the fastest and how many lines we could do a day. We were paid for lines we thinned out.

Sometimes I was in a hurry and carelessly swiped away, not seven inches, but fourteen inches of little plants in a row. I remember, no matter how hard I tried, I could never put back the tender, sugar beet plant once it had been pulled up. We always seemed to have enough plump, sugar beets to send with the buyer to the sugar factory each year.

Most of the money I made went to buy a red, 3-D View Master and their picture reels. The View Master was like a pair of binoculars you put to your eyes. You put in a reel of slide pictures and when you looked inside, the slide pictures lit up as if you were there.

I loved the picture reels of foreign countries, like Hawaii, Switzerland and Sweden! Grace Kelly's wedding in Monaco was also amazing.

COWS IN THE MEADOW

It was always a chaotic day when the cows were let out from the dairy barn for the first time in early summer.

Little Hagar

Many times they ran out wild and dizzy from all the bright sunlight and new freedom.

They had been cooped up in the barn all winter long. We children had to hinder the cows from rushing into Mama's vegetable and flower garden. It was a job to get them all caught and led to the meadow. The cows enjoyed all the good, fresh grass and the abundance of yellow dandelions.

Once when Ingmar was little, a bull rushed him. It became such an upheaval that our little *deja* (day-yuh) milkmaid was fired (against Mama's wishes). Ingmar was a little bloody, but safe. That was a blessing.

•3• EARLY SPRING

Hurrying Through the Snow After a Sauna

Saturday was a fun day! All the work on the farm was done and it was time to heat up the sauna for a steam bath! We carried large bundles of wood from the woodshed to the log house that was our sauna. Then we lit the fire under the oven and under the big hot water kettle. It took many hours to get the temperature hot enough, but it was worth it.

Grandma had made some bundles of birch tree branches with which to swat ourselves. We dipped them first in warm water and then we began to swat ourselves until our skin was red and our pores were opened. Green leaves were flying everywhere!

Now and then we threw a dipper-full of water on the sizzling stones of the oven to get some more really good steam going. This weekly deep cleansing after all our hard work was good for both body and soul, people used to say.

THE SAUNA ROOMS

The Sauna Room

In the southwest corner of the yard, sat our yellow, log sauna. Our sauna had three rooms. There was a sauna room, a laundry room and a dressing room.

The sauna room had a wood burning oven, a huge, hot water kettle and a cold water tap with a big, wooden tub underneath it. There were always fresh birch branches in the room. The first ones to take a bath had to replace the

water in the kettle and in the tub and add more wood to the oven.

The Dressing Room

The dressing room walls were made of heavy logs and the floor of wooden boards. Mama had put her old, hand-woven, carpet runners on the floor to keep out the chill that seeped through the cracks between the boards.

There was a wide bench to sit on. Above it was a wooden rod on which we hung the large linen sheets we used as towels. On the wall was a row of wooden pegs for our clothes.

The Laundry Room

In the laundry room, Mama had a small electric washing machine with a clothes wringer to squeeze the water out. Sometimes we used a metal wash board for the hand washing. The white clothes were cooked in a large kettle to get them extra clean and white.

Papa had designed a rectangular, cement tub for the sauna. In it we soaked and rinsed our laundry. However, when it was really hot in the summer, we children filled the tub with ice-cold water and took a dip to cool off.

We also used this room to cook in. In the summer it was cooler than in the kitchen. We canned fruit and cooked jams and applesauce.

After the slaughter of our pigs in the fall, the big kettle and the stove were heavily used for cleaning and preparing the different food items from the pig.

SAUNA BABIES

My Grandma and Grandpa were the first to take a sauna bath. When we were small, Mama washed our hair and scrubbed us clean. A couple of buckets of warm water over our heads when we were done felt so good.

After the sauna bath we were often so tired, Papa had to wrap us in big linen sheets and carry us to the house.

When we were older, I remember my sister and I, plunging through the snow, in our hurry to get to the house and out of the cold. When we got inside, Mama had tea and sandwiches waiting for us. They were made with Mama's wonderful crusty bread and hardboiled eggs. It was delicious. We fell asleep very clean and tired and cozy with a wonderful feeling of well-being.

Once I had a very embarrassing episode after the sauna. (I was perhaps 4 years old.) I came dancing into the kitchen and flung my bath sheet to the floor. Just then I

noticed a neighbor lady visiting us. I was so ashamed of myself that I ran and hid. I did not come out until after the lady had left even though she assured me that I was very cute.

SISTER MARGARETA

Margareta sister was my model in everything. She was very capable and industrious, and responsible already as a little girl.

Margareta had long, curly, thick hair and great big, brown eyes with long eyelashes. She loved to play hospital. She was always the nurse and I had to be the patient. (When Margareta grew up, she became a neonatal, intensive care nurse.)

I had 'nail straight,' thin hair with small, dark eyes and short eyelashes--to my sorrow. I admired my older sister very much, even if she was bossy at times. Mostly, I was happy to be the little sister.

OUR GIRLS' ROOM

Margareta and I shared a room. Faint, rose-and-white checkered wallpaper ornamented the interior. Two, white, iron beds faced each other from across the room, covered in midnight blue, bed spreads. Underneath our

only window, stood a huge, white desk. Only one of us could use it at a time.

A heavy, blue rug with red and white sprinkles covered almost the entire floor. In the corner by the door stood the ceiling-high, covered fireplace that kept us warm in the sub-zero Finnish winters. Opposite the desk rested a matching, large, white dresser which we also shared.

Margareta and I talked about everything, often late into the night. We loved our cozy, girls' room. Many times we had to spend weeks there in bed because of some childhood illness such as mumps or whooping cough.

GIRLS' CLOTHES

When we were small, Margareta and I often had similar clothes but in different colors.

Once we had on red, velvet coats with brass décor. After a Lutheran church service one morning, a man came up to us and said he admired our family. He thought the girls' little, red coats were especially dear.

I remember the dresses we wore once on a visit to Bjurböle (Byur-beh-lay) in Borgå (Borgo) (sponsored by The Martha Organization). Margareta's dress was eggshell blue with a wide flower garland on the hem and

Early Spring

mine was yellow with the same flower garland on the hem. The ladies thought we looked like butterflies.

EASTER TIME

Mama was very particular about how we were to celebrate the week of Easter. All the work and preparations were to be done before Good Friday (the Friday before Easter Sunday), and on that day, we did not do any work.

On that Friday, we were to think about Jesus and mourn for all our sin which Jesus carried on the cross for us. Then on Easter Sunday we got to celebrate His resurrection and victory over all our sin.

On the afternoon before Easter, the tradition was to place our hats upside down on the big table in the veranda to see what might be left in them later.

We were so excited when we discovered what was put into our hats. Usually we found a large, chocolate egg wrapped in colorful foil with a trinket inside, like a play ring or a small toy. In our hats were also candy eggs, small jelly beans called pologryn (pol-o-grin) and always a large orange.

THE GUESTROOM

Sometimes on Easter, my relatives came to visit. There were Uncle Edvin, his wife Aunt Darling, Cousin Viola and sometimes Cousin Nils. We prepared our best guestroom for them.

The guestroom had a large bed and an oval table with four chairs. A large wardrobe and wash stand filled out the room, all made of the same, beautiful, dark, shiny wood. The bed could be pulled out when needed and pushed back together again while not in use.

The lampshade in the ceiling was most memorable. It was made of green beads and clear beads on multiple strands. The room felt like a lovely, summer day.

It was wonderful to have our relatives visiting. Uncle Edvin was so funny! He was an elementary school teacher and we children flocked around him to hear his funny jokes. His wife, Aunt Darling, was also an elementary school teacher, she was quiet, sweet and mild.

EASTER DINNER

When it was time, everyone gathered in our large holiday decked kitchen. We all fit around our round table and we began the Easter meal.

Early Spring

We children were allowed to eat as many smoked and boiled hotdogs as we wished. We gobbled them down with sweet mustard, mashed potatoes and even hard-boiled eggs. The adults had kallops, a dish of tender chunks of beef in a savory gravy. For dessert we had the traditional memma with sugar and heavy cream.

Memma was a dessert made of rye flour, malt, syrup and chopped, cooked, orange rinds. It was originally baked for hours in large wood ovens, in rectangular forms made of birch bark. Memma tasted like thick, sweet pudding with orange flavoring. Served cold and with heavy, cream, it was delicious! (However, it looked like cow dung.)

INGMAR'S SPRING GAMES

Early in the spring, Ingmar challenged us siblings and his buddies to do sports activities. We began by jumping a rope and practiced another jumping game which we called *Kinkka*. With a stick in the sand, we drew a small obstacle course that we jumped through without pausing.

We also ran one hundred meter races and relay runs while Ingmar just stood and timed us with a stopwatch. He set up a high jump stand that we practiced on frequently. We also played soccer when we had lots of friends visiting at the same time.

Barsas Gården

OVER THE SEAS TO LILLÄNGARNA

Margaretha Lindholm was my best friend. Away from home, we often pretended that we were housewives with many children. I called myself "Brita." We travelled now and then to different countries, to large rocks in our fields.

Our favorite place was Lillängarna (Lil-AYNG-arna), a land of hills and water gardens. We packed a snack of carrots and apples and maybe some pieces of bread and cubes of sugar. When we finally arrived at our destination, you could see a beautiful meadow with islands of water surrounded by tufts of grass.

We pretended every tuft represented a country and the waters were oceans. I imagined we were going on an exciting journey seeing the world. I felt like a giant hopping around the globe-from Finland to Russia to China to India to Italy to Africa and then from Canada to North America and South America, over to England, Greenland, Iceland and finally back home to Finnish Lapland.

We got really exhausted from all that globetrotting, so our bags of snacks came in handy. From previous experience, we had learned that it took a lot of energy just to walk to Lillängarna, much less hop around its globe of waters. It

was worth all the effort though, to play at our favorite spot.

In the hot summertime, the Lillängarna meadow became so dry that horses could graze there. In the fall the heavy rains transformed Lillängarna to a shallow lake. In the winter the lake froze to a fantastic ice skating rink. The boys in the village played ice hockey there while the girls of the village mainly ice skated in Lovisa.

Barsas Gården

•4• The BARSAS FAMILY

GRANDFATHER IVAR

When Mama used to say, "Grandpa is coming!" we children timed it so that when he opened the door we all threw ourselves into his arms.

Grandpa used to play with us in the kitchen. He would sit on the sofa and Grandpa let us take turns standing on his feet. We would hold onto his hands as he said this nursery rhyme, and in the end, he would kick out his legs, which would lift us high up into the air. It was so much fun, we wanted Grandpa to do it over and over again. He used to quote this old children's song:

> Rida, rida ranka,
> Hästen heter Blanka (White)
> Liten pilt så snäll och rar,
> Ännu inga sporrar har.
> När han dem har vunnit,
> Barndoms ro försvunnit.

> Ride, ride, your wooden mare
> The horse's name is Blanka (White)
> My little chap so sweet and dear,
> Still no spurs does he bear.
> When them he has won,
> Childhood's peace is gone.

Grandpa Ivar was very kind even though he often looked serious and a little sad.

THE FOUR DAUGHTERS

My Grandpa Ivar and Grandma Klara (Papa's Mama and Papa) had two pairs of twin girls--four daughters in all. They became my Aunt Signe (Sing-nay), Aunt Gurli, Aunt Eva and Aunt Birgit.

Aunt Signe became an elementary school teacher in Särklax (Sark-lax). Her twin sister, Aunt Gurli, with the beautiful, dark, red hair, married a master of speech and poetry. She did not have an easy life. Her poetic husband turned out to be a con man.

Aunt Eva took care of her mother and father late in life and Aunt Birgit married a dashing, successful farmer. She had two children. These were my cousins—Cousin Åke (Aw-kay) and Cousin Gunvor (Goon-ver).

Margareta loved to be together with Aunt Signe, especially when she got to stay and help in her classroom at school.

The Barsas Family

GRANLIDEN: Grandma Klara's House

Grandpa Ivar and Grandma Klara lived in Granliden (meaning: fir grove), Grandma Klara's charming, two-story house. Aunt Eva lived there as well.

In the summertime, Aunt Birgit and her husband, Uncle Sigurd, came to visit. They brought their children so we could all play together.

All of us cousins had so much fun! Often we were running in and out and upstairs and downstairs and explored all the grounds at Grandma's house. Sometimes we girls hid from the boys and vice versa.

Grandma's long shed had great places to play in. There was a wood shed, a tool shed, an outdoor toilet and an old pigsty. Behind the shed was a hedge with four, tall, fir trees and a smaller hedge of Hawthorne.

In the springtime, the tulips, narcissuses, grape hyacinths and yellow Margareta daisies bloomed. Later, the flower beds glowed with large, orange poppies, white daisies and large, blue, bachelor's buttons flowers.

Upstairs in the house were four, long, attic closets with slanted roofs full of interesting objects. Tucked away was old furniture, fancy clothes, books, magazines, paintings, suitcases, purses and interesting old letters to read. I fought back a little fear creeping through all the ancient stuff. Sometimes it felt as if an invisible being or spirit was present.

Grandma's cellar was dark and unpleasant with steep cement stairs. When it flooded in the spring, we had to drain a whole lot of water because of the snowmelt. The cellar was Grandma's refrigerator. She kept her food cold on the steps leading down to the cellar.

GRANDMA'S GARDEN HARVEST

Grandma Klara harvested from red and yellow, cinnamon apple trees as well as a couple of winter apple trees. Under those trees, a large strawberry patch displayed itself with sweet, wonderful berries. I got to pick the strawberries which Aunt Eva sold to neighbors.

The winter apples were picked last. We wrapped them in newspapers, packed them in boxes and carried them up to the attic. They only tasted sweet after the apples had been wrapped up and given time to ripen during the long, cold winter.

RESCUED:
The Threshing Barn Story

As children, we liked to play in the large, threshing barn close to Granliden. One day Margareta and I were jumping in and sliding down a large stack of straw there. All of a sudden, we fell right through the middle of the stack to the bottom.

We tried to climb up, but the straw was too slippery. We kept sliding back down. We shouted and shouted for help. As if by a miracle, Papa heard our cries and came to our rescue.

PAPA

I often identified with one of Papa's jokes. There was a student in school who kept repeating, "The salmon is a fish. The salmon is a fish. The salmon is a fish. I'm never going to get it!" He would say this information over and over but could not remember it.

I often repeated my homework like that. I was thinking of a million other things while I studied, so I could not remember what I was trying to learn.

Homework seemed so hard, especially my Finnish homework. (One example of a hard Finnish word is *Objektiviteettiperiaate*, "...of objectivity," or

Keskuskauppakamari meaning, "Central Chamber of Commerce.")

I liked to hear Papa sing songs for us. The sad ballad, "The Sorrow of the Mallard," was one of my favorites, but it always made me cry. Papa also sang, *Hey Oho Jungman Jahnson* (Sailor Janson) and many other folk songs.

SUNDAY SCHOOL AT AUNT EVA'S

My parents always honored Sunday. No labor was allowed because it was a day of rest—for both body and soul. We children went to Sunday school in the morning.

My first Sunday school teacher was my own Aunt Eva. I was allowed to help her gather the children by ringing a large, cow bell. We all came in and sat down in Aunt Eva's sal (living room). There were about five children from the village in the Sunday school.

Aunt Eva welcomed everyone. Then she sat down at the piano and we sang some songs in a very high octave. We sang "Children of our Heavenly Father," and, "Be Careful Little Eyes What You See." Songs where we could use our hands and feet were also popular.

Aunt Eva was sick. She had a heart condition which made her very weak. She often burst out weeping when she had hurt feelings. I visited my Grandma and Aunt Eva every day. I loved them both so much. I felt at home in their cozy, orderly home, with antique furniture, nice paintings and ticking clocks.

We went to Sunday school in Köpbacka (Chur-bawcka) when Aunt Eva became too weak to continue. The Sunday school was held in Aunt Sissi's home. She gave us very beautiful greeting cards from America. Even though I was so little, I still remember how joyful and kind she was. Her whole face was squinted up and she made a little jump whenever she was excited.

For many years after, we had Mrs. Ek as our Sunday school teacher. We gathered at the Köpbacka Elementary School. I admired her very much. She told us stories from Jesus' life in such a real and living way. She even used a flannelgraph. (A flannelgraph is a storyboard where pictures, specially coated on the back, stick to the flannel material on the board.)

SUNDAY SCHOOL FOR ALL

God touched my life in such a way that when I became a little older, I also taught Sunday school.

I saw God as an ecumenical God and therefore offered to teach Sunday school in the Lutheran church--the Methodist church and the Pentecostal church. I wanted

everyone to know Jesus and for all the believers to really work together.

After a while, it became too big of a commitment for me so Mama decided to help. She took over teaching Sunday school at the Lutheran church in Köpbacka for the next ten years.

Mama taught the children to pray for their siblings and their parents. She also taught them to be thankful. Mama wanted Jesus to become a friend whom they could talk to all the time, wherever they walked or played or worked.

Many children, besides Mama's grandchildren, had the joy of having Mama Herdis teach them Sunday school.

The Dairy Barn

•5• DAIRY BUILDINGS

Most of the food that we ate, we produced ourselves on the farm. Papa planted oats and wheat and rye early in the springtime. It was always exciting to discover the first, small sprouts of plants.

We worried sometimes about the weather. It was just to pray that we would have enough sunshine and rain--not too much and not too little--for the crops to grow. God took care of us every time.

The Hayloft

The Hayloft was in the attic of the dairy. A long bridge led up to the hayloft on the outside. We children liked to play Hide and Seek among the fancy, old sleds stored there. Hay and straw for the animals was packed up to the ceiling along the walls.

Sometimes we discovered newborn kittens in the hay. They were so cute and helpless with their eyes still closed and ears slicked back. The mama kitty was always close by watching over her brood when we were holding them.

The Outhouse

At one end of the dairy was our outhouse. It was next door to the stench of the dunghill from the animals. It had whitewashed walls which we decorated with beautiful pages out of women's magazines.

In the wintertime, it was freezing cold. As small children, we usually used a toilet chamber pot early in the morning and late at night. We finally got an indoor toilet right before I started jr. high school.

The Dairy Buildings

The Hen House

Hen House

In a room on the right was a henhouse. There were nests all along a wall for the hens to lay their eggs. Close to the ceiling were a couple of poles laid across where the hens and the rooster could sit.

The rooster was fierce. I had heart palpitations just trying to snatch the eggs from the nests before the rooster attacked me.

The Feeding Station

Next to the henhouse was a room with a long table made of cement. When a trap door was unlatched above, hay came down from the hayloft onto the cement table for the

cows. We always had half a dozen or more cows and a couple of calves. In the pigsty were two pigs.

The Stable

In the stable next door, stood one or two horses and sometimes sheep. The harnesses for the horses were neatly hung on a wall. In a section of the stable, Papa had a wood-working shop. There was a long, wooden work bench, tools and wood pieces.

The Storage Area

Next door was the large stable shed, a storage area for some of the wagons and sleds. There was also a place to sharpen our tools. I helped to turn the crank of the sandstone wheel on which Papa used to sharpen his tools.

In one corner, we stored a large heap of rutabagas and turnips. Papa sometimes chopped them in pieces with a sharp blade on a pole. They were a treat for the animals. We children sometimes snacked on them too.

The Clean Room

Next was a small, separate, clean room for straining the milk, before it was poured into big, metal cans. The farmers in the village took turns delivering the milk cans to the dairy in Lovisa.

The Dairy Buildings

One or more of our cats--once we counted sixteen--were always waiting for a bowl of warm milk. Mama portioned out the milk for them in the morning and in the evening.

We had a hand-cranked machine that separated milk from cream. If we turned the cream for a long time, it turned into butter. (If we only would have added sugar to the cream and turned it in a bucket of ice, it would have turned into ice cream.)

Connected to the stable was a lengthy building with different sheds. In one of them sat our tractor and other farm equipment along with big drums of petroleum and oil to fuel the machine.

Falling in the Woodshed

The Dairy Buildings

The Woodshed

Another room in the barn was a large woodshed with an attic. Out of curiosity one day, I climbed the ladder to see what was up in the attic. Up there I saw a low space with a window where Papa stored our skis and poles and sleds.

When I climbed down again, I missed a rung and did a somersault on the ladder. I was left hanging upside down. I thought I was going to die! I yelled and yelled for help and as if by a miracle, Papa heard me! He came running to my rescue and lifted me down. How thankful I was for Papa.

The Millhouse

Next to the woodshed was a millhouse. Papa used to grind grain in a large mill powered by electricity. You walked up the steps to a large funnel where the kernels of seeds were poured. The loud grinder started and the kernels were crushed into flour. Flour dust flew everywhere!

I liked the smell of the warm, freshly-ground flour. We used the mill to mostly make flour for the animals, because the flour was rather coarse for eating. Neighbors also came to grind their grains at our mill.

Meat Storage

In another room was our meat storage. There we had big bins full of coarse salt brine for salt pork, sill (fish) and salted herring. On a large butcher block we carved the meat. The meat storage room always stayed cool. It smelled so good--especially from the delicious, smoked hams hanging from the ceiling.

The Servant's Quarters

The last room was a little private bedroom for a servant. It had a covered fireplace and a small window. When I was six it was made into my playhouse, and when I was twelve it became my art studio.

Grain Storage

At the end of the building was a storage room with wooden compartments for grains like wheat, oats, rye, and dried green peas. As children, we played in the grain (since it would be cooked later.) Now and then we found a mouse in the grain. Sometimes the mouse was dead, but sometimes the mouse was alive! It was really good to have so many cats at Barsas Gården to keep the mice away.

The Dairy Buildings

Above the Gable

On the roof above the gable of the servant's room was a weathervane on a long pole. It looked like a crowing rooster. Underneath the rooster was a plaque with the year of the newly built farm, 1905.

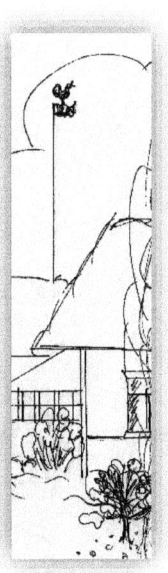

Barsas Gården

•6• MEMORIES OF DEATHS IN THE FAMILY

In a home you experience sorrow and joy, even as a little child. Many in our family were old and sick when we were children. It felt as if we were dealing with death again and again even before my elementary school years. It felt ongoing.

AUNT BETTY

Papa's Aunt Betty lived with Grandma and Grandpa. "She was truly a good and God-fearing woman," my mother used to say. Mama told me that it was Aunt Betty who wanted me to be named "Hagar."

Aunt Betty took care of all the dirty dishes and the picking of weeds--even the stinging nettles--when she stayed with Grandma and Grandpa. She was so diligent to rid them from the property that she had fallen into a patch of them. Ingmar found her almost dead by the side of the ditch. She did die three days later, but she was an old woman though and full of years.

BREAKFAST IN BED FOR AUNT SIGNE

I remember Aunt Signe (Signay) celebrating her birthday in Räfsby. We made her a traditional, Finnish, birthday breakfast tray with a card and some flowers. Then Grandpa, Grandma, Aunt Eva and I stood behind her door singing, "Happy birthday to you, happy birthday to you, happy birthday, dear Signe, happy bir…" Aunt Eva opened the door and dropped the tray to the floor. With a horrified expression, she turned around and cried, "Signe is dead!" Aunt Signe had died on her birthday. She had just turned forty-four.

GRANDPA IVAR'S TIME

Then it was my Grandpa Ivar's turn. I think Grandpa was buried on my birthday. Papa had reserved a private bus for friends and neighbors in our village. Those who wanted to honor the memory of my Grandpa could attend the funeral in the church in Pernå. Pernå was thirty minutes out of Lovisa.

I remember that I was allowed to pick the spring flowers from Grandma's garden. With a bouquet of narcissus and tulips and forget-me-nots, I ran to the bus parked on the Räfsby roadway. With these spring flowers, I was going to honor my Grandpa.

Gurli, my aunt with the beautiful, dark red hair, was the next one to die.

AUNT EVA AND THE ANGELS OF LIFE AND DEATH

I knew that my Aunt Eva might die at any time. She was very ill and in the hospital. One night while she was there, she had a vision.

She saw two people, a dark person and a light person, battling each other. It seemed the light person represented the Angel of Life and the dark person represented the Angel of Death. The light person won. It must have been the Angel of Life for Aunt Eva did not die at that time.

WHEN I DIDN'T FEAR DEATH ANYMORE

When it was finally Aunt Eva's time to die. I became very fearful of death. I feared God most of all. He could snuff out the life of anyone, anytime, anywhere.

I had seen dead people lie on their backs, so for years I would not sleep on my back in case I would die next. I was very much afraid of dying. I thought about the open graves I had seen. What if I was buried alive in one of those coffins?

When I received Jesus Christ as my personal Savior, I was not scared of death anymore. Even if I died, I knew I would go to heaven.

I began praying and talking to God as to my living and loving, Heavenly Father and friend. I began to really believe He was with me and believe His promises in the Bible were true. He promised that when we die, if we had accepted Him into our heart as our Savior, we would be with Him forever. We would never be alone and would never have to be afraid of dying.

SINGING AT THE GRAVE

The ancient, gray stone church in Pernå has witnessed many joyful--but mostly grievous--events in our family. Once though, we had a very embarrassing event at a funeral.

Everyone sings at the open grave during a funeral, with the priest leading. While everyone else was singing along with the priest, Grandma Klara, who was hard of hearing, was singing a whole verse behind everyone else.

All of us children exploded in laughter. We got so hysterical, from the tension and grief of all the deaths in the family, and laughed so hard, we had to be ushered away from the ceremony. It is said, tears and laughter are two sides of the same coin.

Barsas Gården

GRANDMA KLARA COMES TO STAY

After Aunt Eva's death, Grandma Klara moved into Barsas Gården with our family. She was now bent over at the waist and had dementia. (This is where you forget all kinds of things.) We tried to help her. Mama and Papa cared for her wonderfully even when she kept them awake during the night.

Herbert, my younger brother, became best of friends with Grandma. One day, Herbert and Grandma ran away from home.

They took off, wandering the village, looking for Grandma's childhood home. They went to find Haddom which was ten miles away. When the neighbors saw them, they called Mama and she came and got them.

Once she started a fire in the cupboards. When someone asked her about it, she said, "Free from me!" which meant, "Don't look at me." (I didn't do it.) She sewed newspapers onto the hems of her dresses and then told everyone Mama had taught her how to do it.

We were respectful of our grandparents, but sometimes we could not help but laugh because of all the funny things Grandma Klara did.

Memories

Grandma Klara and Herbert Looking for Haddom

Barsas Gården

Memories

Little Critter Funeral

LITTLE CRITTERS

As children, now and then we found a dead bird or hedgehog. When we did, we would fetch the hand cart, lift the dead animal onto it, and the funeral procession would begin.

We would dig a little grave under the svineapple tree. There we put the little animal. After that we filled the

grave, placed some flowers on the mound and made a little cross of sticks to mark it. We sang a song and said a prayer exactly as we had seen a priest do. It was very *sorgligt* (sore-licked) sad.

BANQUETS AND FEASTS

We did not just have big gatherings at our home for funerals but also for the traditional, S.K. Lutheran Reading Questionaire meetings, and prominent 50th and 60th-year birthday parties. Mama Herdis, who was a home economics teacher, knew how to prepare for banquets.

First of all we had to clean and dust and polish the whole house. After that was done, we ironed linen table cloths and put out the best china plates and cups. Silver serving trays and silverware had to be polished. Everything had to shine.

My favorite job after all the cleaning was done was to pick ample amounts of flowers for the house. I designed fantastic bouquets and filled vase upon vase with them. I especially put the vases in our large 'sal' (living room) and dining room. The rooms were permeated with the fresh fragrance of summer.

Every time we had a banquet, for days, our good neighbor, Aunt Sylvi, helped us. Aunt Sylvi was head chef

for the hospital kitchen in Lovisa. She was also a master baker and cake decorator.

It was mind-boggling for us children to see the massive amount of cardamom braided bread, cakes, tortes and cookies that came out of the ovens when we prepared for a banquet. Often there were dozens of trays with salty, open-faced sandwiches.

We children ran around in anticipation of the event and bothered the adults working. We could hardly wait to taste all the sumptuous delicacies.

THE WISDOM OF CHILDREN

At my christening ceremony, a curious lady asked my sister, Margareta, "What is your little sister going to be called?" Although she already knew that my name would be, "Hagar," Margareta very firmly answered, "That, the prost (vicar) will tell us."

When the conversation was on love, Hagar, 4 years old, declared without hesitation her love for, "--only Gert and Reverend Glader."

Ingmar liked to make up rather unique poetry. To Margareta's annoyance, in her memory poem book he once wrote, "The life goes criss and cross, in spite of it

not being the last egg in the frying pan," along with many more worse poems.

When Papa's Aunt was visiting from Helsinki, she asked Herbert, "What do the cats do in the litterbox?" Little Herbert, who was usually very quiet, said with indignation, "But don't you know? That is where the cats go to the bathroom!" (Herbert used much cruder words.) Aunt Agnes could not stop laughing at Herbert's funny answer.

SONGS OF PRAISE

As a child, I designed small bouquets of red clover, white daisies, yellow buttercups and blue cornflowers to give to Mama and my Grandma and my Aunt Eva. I loved to pick wild flowers by the country roads around our farm.

While I picked these flowers, I made up little songs. They came out sounding like different languages, sometimes Italian, Spanish, French, German or Russian. The tunes were so beautiful, tears often streamed down my cheeks when I sang them. I felt so happy. I wondered where all these songs came from.

From a young age, I had been taught about God. Much later, I understood that when I sang, my heart was trying to express my love and thankfulness to God, my Father and Jesus, my Savior and friend. My own little vocabulary didn't have the words but my Heavenly Father

Memories

understood. He understands the language of the heart even from a four-year-old girl.

Wildflowers

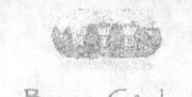
Barsas Gården

•7• MIDSOMMAR

Birch Branch Hunting

SUMMER IN FINLAND

Finland has a long, dark, cold season--almost nine months long. We make up for it in the summertime though with lots of parties and outings and ice cream because the sun does not go down until midnight. Even then, the sun does not completely set. The sky looks like twilight.

It was difficult to sleep because of the light and the heat. The flies and the mosquitos also bothered us. I used to stay awake and read books into the early morning hours.

I borrowed ten to twenty books a week from the library in Lovisa. My ritual was to pick a basket of apples when they were ripe and munch on them while I read during the night until the basket was empty.

We felt so sorry for Mama and Papa who had to get up at 6 am to tend to the animals. Papa talked in his sleep. (He explained that he never got a turn to talk during the day with three women in the house.)

Papa also walked in his sleep. Once he wandered up into the attic and fell asleep there. Mama must have wondered where he was in the morning.

SUMMER PARTY:
Mama's City Friends Visit from Lovisa

Mama hosted a yearly party to kick off the summer. It was mainly for her dear friends at The Martha Organization from when she was working as a consultant in Lovisa.

Some of the ladies were elderly. They often arrived in style in a taxi. Mama was the perfect hostess, greeting each guest with such love and appreciation and grace.

There were Essi Knuts, Elin Dumell, Agda Maria Strandvik, Tora Hildebrand, Aunt Linda and maybe a few more.

Mama actually lived with her friend Agda Maria before she was married to Papa. In the wintertime Mama lived indoors, but in the summertime, she stayed in a playhouse in the front yard.

Agda Maria jokingly said that she should have been called Mama's mother-in-law. She chaperoned the courtship of my Mama and Papa.

Before the guests arrived, we raked the sand pathway leading up to the main entry. We girls cleaned and polished everything, everywhere, until the house was fresh and lovely. As was my habit, I filled the house with beautiful, fragrant flowers.

We children were dressed up for the occasion and lined up to welcome the ladies. Us girls took each lady in hand and curtsied before her. The boys took the ladies in hand and bowed before them. The ladies thought we had grown so much and that we all were such darlings.

After the greetings, we were ushered away from the party but might have some dessert when it was over. We had no idea what Mama and the ladies discussed, but we did

know they were feasting on all the delicacies Mama had prepared for them.

BAKING! BAKING! BAKING!

Mama was a wonderful cook and baked an array of mouth-watering pastries. Mama sometimes baked cream puffs and butter horns, Alexander Squares and Tosca Squares.

She baked small, bitter almond tarts with nut filling, jelly donuts, cinnamon rolls, jellyrolls and fantastic tortes. Some she filled and decorated with fruit and jelly, some with buttercream and some with mocha cream.

There was a chocolate torte with layers of real whipped cream and sliced bananas between them, covered with MORE whipped cream. This was my favorite! Everything was delicious.

The Alexander Squares were topped with royal pink icing and tasted like layers of soft sugar cookies with apple butter in between them.

I started helping my Mama bake Tosca Squares when I was seven years old because I liked them so much.

For these, first I baked a rather thin layer of dough in a jellyroll pan. In a saucepan, I cooked honey and butter and sliced almonds to make a thick topping to spread over

the dough. After the topping received a beautiful, glossy brown color in the oven, the Tosca bites were done.

(See next page for recipe)

Barsas Gården

Tosca Cake Recipe

Tosca Cake

½ cup melted butter
1 cup sugar
2 eggs
2 tbsp milk
2 tsp baking powder
1 cup flour

Mix the melted butter and sugar well with a mixer. Add the eggs one at a time. Add the other ingredients to the batter gradually, stirring slowly. Pour batter into a well-greased 9x13 inch pan. Bake for 15 to 20 minutes at 375 degrees. Pop it out of the pan or leave it in the pan until finished frosting.

Frosting

¾ cup butter
½ cup honey
1 ½ cups chopped or slivered almonds

Boil the ingredients for the frosting in a saucepan until it bubbles and gets slightly sticky. Pour over the cake and bake for another 10 minutes until the frosting is light brown. Take it out and let it cool. Cut it into squares and eat with delight!

Midsommar

BIRCH BRANCH HUNTING

In the end of June, Finland's funnest summer holiday, Midsommar, comes around! It's a day to celebrate the beginning of sun and summer again in Finland and to be out in nature.

The sun was shining high and little white clouds sailed slowly over the clear blue sky. Papa Henning had gathered his children for an outing to Viderbäcken, (Vee-der-bawck-en), our property in the forest. We were going to fetch some young birch trees to decorate our home with for the Midsommar.

Poju (Po-yu), our horse, was trotting merrily in front of our rubber-wheeled wagon. We covered our noses when Poju let out gas. We shouted; "Uj, uj, (Ew! Ew!) Poju, you smell really bad!"

The wagon had only one board to sit on. We children had to stand up and hang onto the wooden pegs on the sides of the wagon. We could also sit at the back of the wagon and dangle our legs over the edge.

Our trip went through the village towards the forest. We children found it interesting when Papa told us who lived in the houses along the way. We knew some of the

children, like Ulla, my friend from school. Her little sister was the first newborn baby that I remember. I was totally taken by how little and lovely she was.

At the Tikander's place we often saw someone in the yard. We liked to play with their four children, Margareta, Nils, Benita and Rolf. Mrs. Tikander was so beautiful and joyful and kind. She even shared her fancy box of chocolates with us children.

We also rode past the Hos farmstead, where Annette and Roger lived with their parents. Their dog bit me once and after that I feared dogs for a long time.

The forest became denser with pines and fir trees. On the ground, we saw large green ferns and lingonberry and blueberry bushes.

Soon we arrived in Viderbäcken and spotted our little log barn at the edge of the meadow.

While Papa and my older brother, Ingmar, were looking for suitable, young, birch trees to chop down, Margareta and Herbert and I took a walk around the meadow.

We tried to find wild, sweet strawberries to thread on long stalks of *timotej*, (tim-o-tay) hay. The snakes liked to sunbathe on the rocks too and hide in the ditches, so we had to pay attention to where we stepped.

Midsommar

Often I would find a grove of fragrant, lily of the valley flowers. I knew Mama would love the bouquet of little, white, bell-like flowers surrounded with green leaves. Mama had them in her wedding bouquet (with long strands of green, asparagus filigree.)

The mini trees were finally loaded onto the wagon and we were on our way home again. We children could now sit among the wonderfully fragrant birches.

The first stop was Grandpa and Grandma's place. We brought them some birches for their home. When we came home, we placed two trees on each side of our own entrances.

The rest we brought inside and placed in the corners of our rooms, to make the home smell like a fragrant, summer forest. It was so festive and delightful to bring a part of nature inside the house.

Mama had cleaned and baked bread and cakes for the holiday. I asked Mama, "Why do we celebrate Midsommar?" She told me, "It is in memory of John the Baptist and Pentecost that we celebrate Midsommar."

SODA POP HEAVEN

Yearly, Papa rode to Vuokkovaara's (Vu-oh-ko-vara 's) Sodapop Factory in Valkom (Val-come). As a tradition, we always bought one or two wooden crates of bubbly, soda pop for everyone to enjoy during Midsommar. The wooden crates were then carefully carried down the steep ladder to our root cellar under the kitchen.

The twenty-four or forty-eight bottles stood shining on the dirt floor. They were filled with ice-cold orange, apple, pear, raspberry, strawberry, lemon and cola-flavored sodas. I scurried up and down the ladder numerous times to taste all the different flavors.

The bottles could be opened and closed again with a special top. We children all got a certain share of the sodas. It was up to each one of us how fast we would drink them.

THE ROOT CELLAR

The root cellar was in the house. It also stored plenty of good food. It had a cupboard full of canned pork chops and ribs. It also had large bins for potatoes, rutabagas, carrots and beets--enough to last the whole year.

Mama prepared lots of good jams, such as: raspberry, blueberry, gooseberry, strawberry and lingonberry jams,

to fill the root cellar. We used them in our pancakes, crepes, cake fillings and porridges.

We steamed red and black currant berries to make concentrated juice in our Mehu Maija steamer. The steamed juice went directly into large numbers of glass bottles.

Later we added water and sugar to the juice to make a concentrated nectar which we called *saft*. We added hot water to it in the wintertime and enjoyed it as a steaming berry cider and added cold water to it in the summertime and enjoyed it as a sweet berry punch.

Barsas Gården

KOKKOS ALONG THE SHORE.

Kokko Fires in Varvet

The Midsommer evening was very exciting. We were usually invited to Aunt Esther's home in Varvet to celebrate and see all the *kokkos* (bon fires) along the shore. Her comfortable and welcoming home overlooked the Bay of Lovisa. Mama had packed some freshly baked bread, cakes and eggs to enjoy at Aunt Esther's with the coffee. We loaded up our rubber-wheeled wagon and off we went.

It took a long time for twilight to come. Slowly the bonfires began to be lit. They fired-up on both sides of the shores along the bay. People decorated their motor

boats with birch branches and the Finnish flag and drove by us waving to everyone on the shore.

The night was so still; you could hear people talking clearly in the boats even though they were far away. The water carried the sound of their voices like a megaphone to the shore.

MY SAD MEMORY

One Midsommar I remember especially. We were not going to celebrate Midsommar in Varvet at Aunt Esther's this year. I was so disappointed. I nagged and begged my parents to go anyway.

Mama and Papa looked at each other so sad and tired. Finally, Papa put me on his bicycle and we rode to Varvet, but there were no *kokko* fires that summer. I was so sad I had made Mama and Papa sad by wanting to get my own way.

Barsas Gården

Midsommar

WORKING IN THE HAY FIELDS

Barsas Gården Hayfields

Once we were out of school for the year, we would help work in the fields. Putting up hay was the next big summer job. We were woken up early at 6 a.m. After a

strong cup of coffee with cream and sugar--and maybe a cardamom bun, we stumbled out into the field.

Sometimes we had to travel by horse and wagon to a hay field further away from our home. We had the help of neighbors who liked to earn a little extra in the summer. The work morale was good and we talked and joked and laughed with one another all day long.

Some of the helpers were from Lovisa. One of them was Dansken, who spoke Danish with us, and Miranda, a beautiful, tall, gypsy girl, and a widowed mother with three children. Several other neighbor ladies with children also came to help.

Papa had cut the hay with a hay cutting machine that Poju, our horse, pulled along. Then Papa connected a large rake to the horse to rake the hay into neat rows.

It was hard work from morning to evening for us girls. When we were teenagers, my sister and I were rather vain. We wanted to get a nice sun tan out in the fields. It backfired a little though. By not being covered properly, we got sunburned--instead of tanned--and suffered the stinging, sharp points of hay whenever it touched our skin.

Our job was to lift suitable piles of hay onto a wooden pole with a pitch fork. The whole field was soon filled

with rows of neat little haystacks. The sun and the wind dried the fresh and fragrant hay after a week or two.

When it was time to bring the hay into the barns, we were recruited again. Equipped with pitch forks we marched to the fields and began lifting the hay off the poles onto a hay wagon. When I was young, Papa used Poju to pull the hay wagon. They stopped at each pole, while we loaded the wagon.

One person had to be on the hay wagon to help pack the hay evenly into a square. When the load was huge, it was driven to the hayloft above our dairy. Papa gathered speed, and with clattering hooves, he and Poju charged up the bridge to the hay loft.

CLATTERING HOOVES

One day we almost had a terrible accident. A neighbor lady with three children was helping us with the hay labor. One of her boys had epileptic fits at times.

Just when Papa was charging up the bridge, this boy ran out from the hay loft and fell with an epileptic fit. His mother ran after him and got him pulled to the side a moment before the horse and the wagon came thundering past them. This boy could have been trampled to death.

Barsas Gården

THE WORK OPTION

If we girls, Margareta and I, did not want to work in the field one day, we could swap with Mama and stay in the kitchen all day long. The workers had to be fed well and at certain intervals. Mama did not mind going out in the field or even into the hayloft. It was hot in the kitchen. There were no fans or air conditioning.

The Coffee Break

At 10 am it was the morning coffee break and both of us girls prepared a basket for the workers with black currant juice and Mama's freshly baked yeast bread with lots of butter. Armed with a large coffee pot and cups and spoons, and cream and sugar, we walked to the field to serve everyone some refreshments.

Middag Lunch

At 12 o'clock sharp, everyone came in from the fields to have a hot, sit-down, middag, lunch. The food was to be good and the food was to be plentiful. For example, we might cook potatoes, meatballs with gravy, pickled cucumbers and beets, and bread and butter, with milk to drink for twelve people.

We then washed all the dishes by hand, dried them and put them away. After that the kitchen was cleaned up and ready for the evening meal. It was stifling hot by this time.

Afternoon Coffee Break

At 3 p.m. it was time for the afternoon coffee break. We served coffee and juice and sweet cinnamon or cardamom buns to the farm helpers.

Now, we also got to take a little break from the kitchen chores. It was so refreshing to sit under a tree in the shade. Sometimes we climbed up on a big rock in the field. We tried to fit as many as possible up on the rock without falling off. We joked and laughed and thought we looked as if we were on a deserted island in the middle of the sea.

The Evening Meal

At 5 p.m. it was time for the evening meal. All the workers came in from the hay fields. Sometimes we served polish sausage cooked in the oven with cheese wedges, served with rice and a thick white sauce flavored with ketchup. Other times we served a delicious meat and vegetable soup. After cooking and washing dishes all day long

Barsas Gården

inside the hot kitchen, we were ready to go out to the hay fields the next day.

• 8 • VISITS WITHIN THE ARCHIPELAGO

Boating in the Archipelago

An archipelago (ark-i-peh-lago) is when you have a big body of water with a lot of islands in it. Finland has many archipelagos. Many people like to buy one of these islands and make a little summer house on it. Then they can visit it when the weather is finally warm and sunny.

A few times we were invited to visit good friends on Trollholmen, an island not far from Lovisa. First we took a bus to Valkom, two miles away. Then we walked to Vårdö (Vordeh) shore, a forty-five-minute walk. There, we were met by either Fjalar (F-yah-lar) or Tage (Taw-gay) with a row boat. Then we were rowed to Trollholmen. (Mama was always afraid to step into a rocking boat.)

Ruth or Beda welcomed us. We liked them all so very much. They were of Aunt Esther's family. Oh, how we

enjoyed jumping off the rocks and swimming by the shore!

They always served fish soup when we visited. It tasted wonderful after we had been out in all the sunshine and sea air. In Finland there is a saying that fish long for water, whether in or out of the water. This is why you are always thirsty after eating seafood.

MAMA GROWING UP IN VESSÖ

My Mama was born on Vessö (Vesseh), which was a large island in Finland. Vessö had a steam boat that left early in the morning for Borgå (Borgo) City. It stopped at many landing places along the way to pick up passengers, large jugs of milk for the dairy, packages and mail. The steamboat came back in the late afternoon, in time for the farmers to milk their cows in the evening.

One of Mama's relatives owned a country store on Vessö. She sold everything from food and clothing, to farm tools and candy. The store was also the local Post Office. The family lived above the store. Therefore, the store was open all hours of the day or night, for the customers knew where to find the owners.

Mama grew up next door to the elementary school. The greatest sorrow for her, her two sisters and four brothers, was that they had such a SHORT walk to school.

In summer times and on important birthdays, we traveled to Vessö. We visited my Aunt Karin and Uncle Gustav and cousins, Nils, Marianne and Birgitta. My Uncle Edvin and Aunt Darling, and cousins, Maj-Britt and Viola, lived nearby too. Aunt Karin and Uncle Edvin were Mama's sister and brother.

It was fun seeing my cousins. We did some sight-seeing around their neighborhoods and explored the forest in between the two homes of our relatives. We skipped ropes, played catching games, 'Last Couple Out' and 'Hide and Seek.'

UNCLE EDVIN & AUNT DARLING

Uncle Edvin and Aunt Darling were teachers in the elementary school in Vessö. They also lived in an apartment attached to the school building. We found it interesting visiting the empty classrooms when school was out.

We checked out the gymnastic room with all the equipment. Long ropes hung from the ceiling which we used to climb. We also sat at the teacher's desk or drew pictures on the large black board.

FRIENDS FROM ÅLAND

We had many fun summer evenings together with a special family. They were three girls in the family and we were two girls and two boys. Their main home was on the delightful island of Åland, a large island between Finland and Sweden. In the summertime, they vacationed in their charming, old fashioned villa in Varvet.

We usually invited them for an evening party at our home. As a custom, we prepared large trays of open-faced sandwiches. On them were cold cuts, decorated with sliced tomatoes, cucumbers and lots of parsley and dill. We also made egg sandwiches with anchovies. Our guests stayed with us until the wee hours of the night laughing and talking about everything.

A NEAR-DROWNING

Once I fell in the bay at Johanson's Bridge and I did not know how to swim. I hollered for help but went under the water again and again while splashing for dear life. The grownups just stood by and watched and even laughed at me. They did not know that I couldn't swim and was drowning.

Even today I still do not like to put my head under the water when I swim. But now I never ignore anyone who looks as if they are in trouble in the water.

Visits Within the Archipelago

INGMAR'S SWIMMING LESSONS

Ingmar had swimming lessons one summer. At the end of the course everyone had to pass a swimming test.

I was really anxious for Ingmar because the test was to rescue a fully-dressed person from drowning. The person he had to rescue was a lady wearing a thick, heavy coat, big, rubber boots and a scarf on her head. My fears were relieved. Ingmar passed his test and did not let anyone drown. (Later I figured that it was another student dressed up like a little old lady.)

After the tests, the whole class paraded down a bridge in a single line past a judge. He placed a wreath of bay leaves on each head, like a victory crown given to an athlete in the Olympics. I was very impressed by the ceremony.

Barsas Gården

ADVENTURE AT SEA

Tarping the Boat During a Sudden Storm in Perna Bay

Papa's cousin, Uncle Erik, his wife, Aunt Ulla, and the second cousins came to visit. They wanted to take a motorboat trip to visit Papa's Uncle John and wife, Anna Barsas, in Pernå at their summerhouse, called Pliggeberg. All of us children were allowed to come along on the boat trip.

All of a sudden, in the middle of the Pernå Bay, a storm came upon us with a downpour of rain. It rained so hard that Uncle Erik had to turn off his boat engine and quickly rig a tarp over us.

Aunt Ulla quickly held me tight. She had such an iron grip around me, I almost suffocated. I think she was very much afraid we would go overboard. I felt totally calm though.

We finally landed, safe and sound. However, I don't know how happy our host and hostess were with our daring visit. As we were ravenously hungry after the storm, the boys cleaned off the cake platter before the adults got to have any of the treats with their coffee.

A SURPRISE VISIT

In the summertime, relatives visit one another, especially for birthdays or weddings. However, one day my Uncle, Reverend Anders-Gustav and his wife, my Aunt Signe (Signay) came to Barsas Gården for a surprise visit.

I was home alone and panicked. Guests had come and I thought I was to take care of them. I did not know where Mama was and when she would be home again. The thought occurred to me, "Maybe the visitors are hungry?" So I did what Mama would do.

I *snabbt* (quickly) ran out to the potato plot and dug-up a pot-full of new potatoes. When the potatoes were scrubbed and boiling on the stove, I climbed down into our cellar to fetch a large, glass jar of canned pork chops.

Thank goodness! Mama had returned. I was a little worried that I had acted in a haste though. While the adults ate, I picked a large bowl of sweet strawberries for dessert. I didn't know I was acting quite grown-up for a six-year-old. (All praise goes to Mama though. From a young age, she trained us to cook, bake, clean and even host visitors.)

My aunt and uncle were so appreciative. My Uncle A.G., especially, loved berries of every kind.

THE SUNBEAM EXPERIENCE

In the summer, my Uncle A.G. (Reverend Uncle Anders-Gustav), Aunt Signe and their children, our cousins, Maj-Gret, (My-gret) Kerstin and Torsten, came to visit us. They often traveled around and held Christian meetings in churches and homes. We participated at a prayer house in Lovisa.

It was wonderful to hear Uncle A.G.'s calm and mighty voice. I also remember how beautifully my aunt and uncle and cousins sang in harmonies. Aunt Signe played the guitar. She taught me a special children's song. One line in it was especially memorable:

"God wants me for a sunbeam, a sunbeam, a sunbeam, a heavenly sunbeam from God."

Later, after I became a believer in Jesus Christ, I heard a voice that sounded like mighty waters from heaven using those exact words. The words so lovingly compelled me: "I WANT YOU TO BE A SUNBEAM FOR ME."

UNCLE OSKAR & AUNT ANNA

Uncle Oskar and Aunt Anna, Papa's Aunt, were often in Lovisa in the summer time. They rented a little house by the elementary school. (It was also the house where our cook lived when I was young.) Aunt Anna was so sweet and mild. Uncle Oskar was funny. We children liked them both so much.

We learned to know their children, Papa's cousins. The boys were Erik, Åke and Holger. The girls were Brynhild (Brin-hild), Anna-Greta and Ulla. We sometimes visited with our relatives in Pålböle (Pohl-beh-lay) and in Illby (Eel-bih) and with our relatives in Grottabacka (Greta-bawcka), but not so often.

HELSINKI VISITORS:
A Can of Pineapple Juice

We children were really happy when two of Grandma's 'so called' relatives, Harry, and his wife, Judith, came to visit.

In Finland, it is customary to bring a nice gift when you come to visit someone, especially if you come unexpectedly or seldom visit. Many people bring a box of chocolates or a bouquet of flowers--something the whole family can enjoy. When Harry and Judith came to visit though, they usually brought a can of pineapple juice.

After a good sauna, Harry and Judith usually had cup of elderberry tea from our own tea leaf bushes. We wondered what that elderberry tea did to him later.

After the tea, Harry got all charged up and had us roaring with laughter as he chased us around the whole house. We all screamed and ran in excitement. Harry and Judith loved children but they could not have any of their own.

A TRAGIC LOVE STORY

When he was young, Harry (who always brought the pineapple juice) had been head-over-heels in love with Magdalena. She was the beautiful and charming daughter of Consul (Ambassador) Fagerlund. Consul Fagerlund's wife was Papa's aunt.

Harry and Magdalena got engaged and were very much in love. At the time, Harry was studying for his doctorate.

Suddenly, Magdalena took ill. She died soon after of cancer. Harry's doctorate had taken a long time to write.

In his sorrow, he threw all his work into the grave with Magdalena. It was a very tragic love story.

Barsas Gården

• 9 • SUMMER FUN

Mama, Margareta and Hagar with Patuna Ladies Washing Carpet Runners.

CARPET WASHING BY THE SEASHORE

At least once every summer, we loaded up all our hand-woven carpet runners to wash by the Patuna seashore.

Mama packed several scrubbing brushes and pine soap with a basket of food for the day. There was a thermos full of hot coffee, cream and sugar, cold soda pop and salami and cheese sandwiches.

We could smell the sea from a long way off. It was mingled with the smell of fish oil from the seafood cannery, Finska Fiskeriet on the shore.

We began by tossing the runners into the sea to soak them. Once in a while a wave took off with one of them, and the bravest of us had to jump in to fetch it.

On a platform floating in the water, we pulled one runner up at a time over a long table. Then we scrubbed it with the pine soap til our backs and shoulders ached. The sun burned above us. We got sunburned even though there were fresh, windy gales cooling us down and tossing our hair.

It was so pleasant to visit and laugh with the other girls and ladies, who also were washing their carpet runners.

Summer Fun

We hung the clean runners on a rack by the shore to dry. A few hours later, at the agreed upon time, Papa came to pick us up in the rubber-wheeled wagon.

We washed our runners by the seashore, because in the deep of winter, when it was cold and dark, the fragrance of pine soap and sea water reminded us of the sunshine and sea breezes of summertime.

AFTER-CHORE SWIM-TIME

After all the chores were done, we children often walked or biked to a sea shore by the railway called Korsvik tvåan. Sometimes our friends, Margaretha and Nisse, came with

Inner-Tubing in Varvet at our Favorite Swimming Hole

Barsas Gårdén

us. They owned a large inner tube which we blew up and we could sit in and float around. When the train happened to come by the seashore, the engineer blew the whistle and waved to us.

SUMMER LUNCHES

Everything Tastes Better Outdoors

Sometimes in the summer, it was so hot that we had our meals in the shade of the house on a narrow lawn. I remember how good the food tasted when we ate it outdoors. We set up a long table and two benches. We would sit and eat salad with lettuce and spinach grown from our own garden.

Summer Fun

Mama made a creamed vegetable soup from all the new little carrots, potatoes, green peas, dill and parsley from the garden. She called it "Glutton's Soup" because you couldn't stop eating it even when you were full. It was that good!

Papa had a good joke. During some lean years, people often went begging for food. Once a beggar came to a farm to ask for something to eat. When he saw that the family was eating salad for dinner, he could not bring himself to ask for anything, as they themselves, were already eating grass.

A TRIP TO HELSINKI

After all our begging and pleading, Mama and Papa finally decided to take us children on a pleasure trip to Helsinki. We were going to Högholmen, the outdoor animal zoo in Helsinki! (Helsinki is the biggest city in Finland and has an interesting mix of new and old buildings.)

To get to there from Barsas Gården, we first took a bus to Lovisa, then another bus to Helsinki, a tram ride to the harbor, and then finally we boarded a little ferry boat. The Helsinki zoo was on an island.

There were some exotic animals, but most of them were sleeping or in hiding. We saw some bears, some deer and some apes. It was fun running around on this little island

looking into the different animal cages, but I felt sorry for the animals, all caged up instead of living free in nature.

Coming back, we were hungry and tired. My sister had a famous saying from that trip: "If I get a hotdog and an ice cream cone, I will be satisfied." Everyone was shocked when she said it. (In our family it was UNHEARD OF to get two treats at the same time.)

It was good that we went to Helsinki that summer, for we never visited Högholmen Zoo again.

MY FAVORITE MOVIE EVER

We did not often see movies in my childhood, but I remember a few. We had two movie theaters in Lovisa, The Sylvia Theatre and The Ulrika Theatre. Once I saw a really funny movie, something like a Charlie Chaplin and once, a romantic comedy with the sweet Romy Schneider. It might have been called *Sissi: The Young Empress.*

The best movie I ever saw though, was The Ten Commandments with Charlton Heston as Moses. I, together with my family--and maybe half of the townspeople of Lovisa--were in a packed-out Ulrika movie theater.

The movie changed my life. I was only, maybe six years old, but I never forgot the burning bush with the voice of

God, or the Death Angel smiting all the first-born sons in Egypt. Then there was the parting of the Red Sea.

It was incredible seeing those huge walls of water standing up while the children of Israel walked through on dry land. They made it to the other side while the Egyptian army all drowned.

Barsas Gården

•10• ELEMENTARY SCHOOL

The Playground

LOVISA SCHOOL LUNCHES

In the beginning of the school year, every student was required to bring two liters of lingonberries to school. The lingonberries collected from all the students were stored in big buckets at the cook's house. They were put in a root cellar underneath her kitchen floor.

You accessed the root cellar by lifting up a hatch in the middle of the floor and climbing down some steps to its lower level. The cook lived in a little house next to the school. There she also cooked our school lunches.

The school cook had to get up early to begin cooking the noon meal in time for lunch. She used a large wood stove. Large pots were used to boil the meat and vegetables or split peas for split pea soup. These were delicious together with some hard rye bread and butter.

We also had rye flour porridges with lingonberries, but they were not my favorite. The macaroni with ground beef gravy was good as well as the hot cream of wheat porridge with cold, berry juice soup. These were very typical Finnish dishes that we children ate.

THE LUNCH DE JOUR

Every student was on a rotating school lunch 'tour of duty,' called a *de jour* (day-joor). A couple of us fetched the piping-hot school lunch and carried the buckets between us. We then portioned it out onto plates waiting on the long, platform tables with benches on both sides.

We usually gave an extra-large portion to our teacher who presided at the head of the table. She always tried to give half of it away to some unlucky student.

Elementary School

The twenty-some first and second graders, with their teacher, marched in first to the dining room. Then a combined class of thirty students in third, fourth and fifth grade came from their classroom. Everyone bowed their heads and together prayed and thanked the Lord for the food we were to receive.

While we were eating, we were supposed to be absolutely quiet. Some boys always tried to stir up trouble by joking and laughing. If they were punished, the younger ones had to go and stand facing a corner in the room. It was very shameful and embarrassing.

The older boys were sent outside into the hallway. Some girls, giggling and sharing secrets, got caught too and were in trouble once in a while.

CLASSES AND GYM

It was fun to learn to read and write and do math. We also had music and a gym class. These were held in the dining room during the cold season. We played baseball in a sports field close by when it warmed up. We had to hike down a steep hill to get there and hike back up again.

I did not like ball games because teams had to be chosen. The clumsy and uncoordinated ones were always picked last. I dreaded the picking order not just for myself but for all the unpopular students whom no one wanted on their team.

As a child, I really felt for any student who was picked-on because they were fat or had bad clothes or were just shy. I wanted to be nice and friendly to the picked-on ones. I felt their anguish.

I had a major crush on a boy. He was blond and blue-eyed, smart and sweet.

MY FAVORITE SUBJECT

My favorite subject was art. I loved to draw and paint. Every year it was thrilling to receive new pens and crayons, notebooks and a tub of a strange-smelling glue at the beginning of each semester. I stored everything in my own desk which we called a 'pulpet'.

In art class, we had different drawing assignments, like painting a fall landscape or drawing a picture of a fun summer event. Every picture was posted on the wall. We then discussed the different works of art and chose our favorite.

It was a little embarrassing that my picture was often chosen, but I had a knack for art. (I didn't always do well in math or science or later on in the difficult Finnish

Elementary School

language classes.) I loved the beautiful colors in art. They made me so happy.

It was peculiar. When everyone else drew fir and pine trees--trees native to Finland--I drew palm trees. They were so cool and intriguing to me.

Later, when I was a grown-up, I got to live in California, in the United States. I saw palm trees every day, and even had two growing in my own back yard!

A FINNISH RECESS

During recess, we played on the monkey bars and the swings. We liked to skip ropes. We jumped rope by ourselves or with two students swinging a long rope between us. Students would take turns jumping in and out of the rope while it was being turned.

We played soccer and catch. Sometimes we played a circle, 'catch me' game. One person would chase another until they were caught or found a safe place in the circle.

Some of us girls liked to play house in a little grove outside the school building. We played among the rocks and lingonberry bushes in the sunshine with the birds chirping, bees humming and ants dragging pine needles up into their anthills.

Barsas Gården

THE DREADED OUTHOUSE

We especially dreaded using the outhouse (the outdoor toilet). There was a boys' outhouse and a girls' outhouse. Each had a communal wooden bench with ten holes of toilet seats in the same room without dividers.

It was hard for us little ones to reach up to the seats. The holes seemed huge. When you looked through the hole you saw a ten-foot drop.

The boys always teased the girls saying they could see us from underneath, but that was not true, of course. Even still, it was sheer terror for us girls to use the outhouse.

Elementary School

THE HEALTH CHECK-UP

In school, we had a health check-up every year. A doctor and a nurse came to the school. We had to strip to our underwear and line up in the gym--the boys and girls together.

It was horrifying and embarrassing. We were scrutinized. Underarms and underwear were checked for signs of puberty. We got tuberculosis tests and shots. I still dread immunizations from those early school experiences.

Barsas Gården

Taking Herbert to School on the Big Bike

BIKING TO SCHOOL WITH HERBERT

I was only eight years old when my younger brother, Herbert, began going to school too. He was a year younger than me.

I learned to ride a bike that year but on a grown-up bicycle. This meant I could take Herbert to school. Since I was so small, I had to peddle standing up the whole time. Herbert sat on the back of the seat of the bike holding on for dear life.

Elementary School

It was so hard to ride him to school every day and back. I peddled the bike as fast as I could to make Herbert hold on tight. I rode over boulders and in deep ruts just to make him suffer. I was so exhausted after riding us both home, I often dropped the bike to the ground and wept.

LITTLE HERBERT

When he was a child, Herbert was so small because he wouldn't eat anything. Mama finally baked him jellyrolls which he liked and Herbert lived on jellyrolls with coffee. It was the only thing that he would eat, but the doctor told Mama it was okay, Herbert would grow up just fine.

Later, Herbert had a terrible accident as a young boy. While sledding down a street he was struck by a car. The boys who were supposed to watch out for danger were not taking their turns. He suffered a severe head trauma that affected him for a long time.

Living on a farm was not easy for him as well. He suffered fierce hay fever during the summer. Sneezing and wheezing, his nose ran all the time because of the cut grass in the air, and his eyes swelled shut.

In spite of all these trials, Herbert was a sweet boy, quiet and content. He grew up to become a tall, handsome mailman who delivered all sorts of mail to the townspeople of Lovisa.

Barsas Gården

•11• IN THE ATTIC

WINTER LAUNDRY

In the wintertime, Mama hung the washed clothes in the unfinished attic. The clothes became stiff in the cold. It took weeks for them to dry. When they were finally dry, they were stiff as sheets of cardboard paper.

Sometimes I made a play house and took care of my little dolls in the attic. We found fancy clothes and played dress up. Old beds and a beautiful, antique, baby carrier of ornamental wrought iron became perfect props for our pretend games.

Some wooden boxes held strange-smelling ointments and herbal medicines. I was a little scared to be alone in the big attic with its dark corners, but the fun of playing there helped me overcome my fears.

IN THE ATTIC:
The Karelian Refugees

After one of the wars in Finland, people from the eastern part, called Karelen (KAH-reh-lane), had to flee from their homes because their territory was given to Russia.

One of these couples from Karelen came to our house for help. We invited them to stay in a heated room in that attic. They lived there for a while until they could move on. The refugees spoke only Finnish and we spoke only Swedish. I felt so sorry for them.

IN THE ATTIC:
Valter Sevelius' Fabric Store

In the year 1880, Finland was still a Grand Duchy of Russia. That meant Russia was ruling over Finland and could make citizens in Finland do whatever they told them to do and Russia told Finland that the young men needed to join their army.

Papa had an uncle named, Valter Sevelius. To avoid having to fight in the Russian Army, he fled to Argentina. Later, when it was safe to return, Valter and his wife, Dagny), set up a fabric store in Hangö.

When they closed their shop, Valter stored his merchandise in our attic. We loved the shiny wooden boxes with glass windows full of laces and fancy beads for dresses. There were ribbons and monograms. All the letters of the Swedish alphabet could be sewn onto clothing.

In the Attic

HAGAR STARTS A BUSINESS

The boxes were so intriguing, just sitting there in our attic. When I was five years old, I packed up small bundles of these special laces, buttons, monograms and ribbons, put them in a large shopping bag, and went door to door selling them.

Our neighbors happily bought my pretty laces and buttons at discount prices. I had earned quite a small sum of change. Then Mama got a phone call from a neighbor wondering if she knew that Hagar had become a sales lady? Mama put a stop to that right quick.

Barsas Gården

Mama as a Martha Consultant

MAMA

Before Mama married Papa, she worked as a consultant for The Martha Organization. Mama had graduated as a teacher from the prestigious Högvalla Home Economics Institute. As part of her training, she worked on large estates as a household advisor.

Mama planned menus and helped cook dinners for barons and their guests when they had large dinner parties. Some estates were even called castles because of their size and appearance. One family owned such a large estate that the children were allowed to bicycle indoors to get from one end of the house to the other.

In the Attic

When Mama was young, these were difficult times for Finland. Finland had endured three different wars by the time my mother married.

Finland's neighbor, Sweden, sent military leaders to help them win the war with Russia. However, the southern part of Finland had to pay an especially heavy price for their help. Finland had to give parts of their land to the Swedish military leaders as a 'thank you'.

The farmers on those lands were required to pay the feudal land owner (the Swedish leader) day labors and produce (food), in return for a little house and a small plot of land.

When the Winter War of 1940 was over, Mama was hired as a consultant to reach out and help the women of the Finnish countryside. She would teach them how to grow healthy vegetables from seeds donated by The Martha Organization.

The Martha Organization was somewhat based on the woman, *Martha*, in the New Testament. She served people in her home with her hands and heart. The Martha Organization wanted to help people with that same spirit.

Miss Herdis (Mama) was hired to travel around East Nyland county (southern Finland), advising housewives on how to grow and care for their gardens. She also gave

home advice on rearing children, how to care for farm animals and of course, how to cook delicious dinners and decorate fancy, many-layered cakes.

They called her Lilla Fröfröken (Lee-lah Fre-frecken) Little Miss Seed, because she handed out so many seeds for vegetable gardens. Mama knew the health benefits of those little gems she passed along. She knew what happened when sun and water were added to them. They grew up into super vegetables. When these vegetables were eaten, they would make the people of her country strong again!

She travelled by bus to the different communities she was assigned to, bringing several, heavy, wooden boxes filled with bags of seeds with her. Someone in every village came to pick her up at the bus stop, often with a horse and buggy or a sled in the winter.

Once in the wintertime, a man came to pick her up with a small sled. He loaded her wooden crates on it. Afterwards, he found there was no room left for my mother, so he plopped her on top of her cargo and off they went.

She was appreciated and loved wherever she went, bringing her good gifts and lovely, capable self.

In the Attic

LOVISA WARTME HISTORY

Mama and Papa met when they were a little older, in their thirties, and married during *The Continuation War* in 1942. There were three wars in Finland from 1917-1945. My mother and father lived through all of them.

Finland suffered the loss of many lives. In every home, someone had to give up a father or a brother or a son. Grief and poverty and famine and sickness were everywhere. Russia was ruling and Finland did not have freedom to do things its own way.

When Ingmar was born, in 1943, food and clothing were obtained by rations (tickets). Everything was saved, like papers and string. Even bark off the trees was mixed with flour to make bread to keep away starvation.

RUSSIAN RULE

We were under Russian rule for many years. Finnish teachers were required to teach students the Russian language. Mama often spoke of *schapushka* (shaw-push-kaw). We understood that it had something to do with food.

We loved the dish called *Russian beef a la stroganoff* (strow-gen-off). It was always cubed, cooked beef in a brown

gravy with cubed, cooked beets. We also talked about *sliscikan*. (I think it was a sled that looked like a row boat.)

We knew the Russian words:

1. *Da* (dah) Yes
2. *Njet* (n-yet) No
3. *Njet polimai parushki.*
   (N-yet pole-ee-my par-oosh-ski)
   I don't speak Russian.
4. *Spasiba* (spa-see-bah) Thank you
5. *Dashvidania* (dah-s-vee-dawn-yah) Goodbye.

RUSSIAN ROYALTY

During the Russian Grand Duchy era from 1809-1917, Lovisa was an idyllic, summer resort town for the Russian royalty. People moved out of their own homes so Russian dignitaries could rent them for the summer. The tsar usually came with his entourage to fish for salmon in the springtime. The sand beaches and the health spas were most popular.

LOVELY LOVISA

Lovisa is beautifully located in Lovisa Bay. Boats of every kind line the bridges by the shores. In the olden days there were steam ships. Large and small sailing ships carried people across the water to Borgå and Helsinki. Some even came from other countries while I grew up. Now, fast motor boats are the favorite way to get around and get to everyone's summer cabin island.

Lovisa is known for its beautiful, cobblestoned, marketplace square. Stately buildings, green parks and large avenues of trees surround it. The market place is used for sales of berries and vegetables, wild mushrooms and fresh fish. Finnish people love fish! Specialty breads and flowers can be bought there too, especially in the summertime.

People from the countryside come very early in the morning to set up their wares and sell their items. Shoppers relax with a cup of coffee and a fresh danish or a jelly donut from the outdoor cafeteria. The ice cream kiosks (kee-osks) are popular too. The usual ice cream flavors are sold, but also uniquely Finnish favorites like pear, black currant, black licorice or black licorice with lemon.

The marketplace has special events. With all the pomp of the Rococo era, Lovisa has a re-enactment of the Swedish King and his entourage's entrance into the city long ago. The city is named after his queen, Queen Lovisa. It was strange, but she never visited the city of which she was the namesake.

Barsas Gården

FORT UNGREN:
The Island Summerfest

Lovisa is surrounded by military forts on land and with one on an island near the city. The largest is on 'Black Island'--a 2-hour boat trip from Lovisa Bay. It is a popular tourist attraction with a massive stone fort.

The walls around are thick and many visitors like to walk on them. The top of the fort has an awe-inspiring view of the bay. Underneath are cave-like rooms you can explore.

In Lovisa, Fort Ungern was used to host the yearly Summerfest put on by the fire department. The season opened with a parade of firemen playing in a brass band. The program was outdoors inside the fort.

Popular singers came and a magician entertained the children. People sat on benches in long rows and visited with friends. Children ran around, playing and participating in small competitions and buying food from the concession stand. The ladies of the firemen served hotdogs and hamburgers and ice cream. Soda and coffee were served too, of course.

There was a dance with a popular orchestra in the pavilion for the young people. Altogether, it was fun and exciting

In the Attic

for people of every age group. People came from far away for this yearly event.

As a child, I remember participating in a music festival held in Fort Ungern. Hundreds of singers paraded into the fort wearing beautiful, national costumes. Every county had its own pattern and color theme.

It was an unforgettable event. Colorful flags fluttered in the wind. Choir after choir sang folksongs. Of course, they always sang, our national anthem, "Our Land, Our Land."

Our Land Our Land

Our land, our land, our fatherland,
Sound loud, O name of worth!
No mount that meets the heaven's band.
No hidden vale, no wave-washed strand.
Is loved, as is our native North.
Our own forefathers' earth.

Thy blossom, in the bud laid low,
Yet ripened shall upspring.
See! From our love once more shall grow
Thy light, thy joy, thy hope, thy glow!
And clearer yet one day shall ring.
The song our land shall sing..

Barsas Gården

•12• CHRISTMAS

HOW TO KILL AND PREPARE A PIG

Already early in the fall we began to prepare for Christmas by butchering our two pigs. A neighbor came to help us kill our loudly squealing pigs.

After the pigs were taken care of, they were hung up and the skin was peeled off with scalding, hot water and a horse shoe. All the innards were taken out and carried in tubs with straw to our bastu (sauna) building, where they were thoroughly cleaned and cooked in large kettles of boiling water.

Everything was used for food. The ribs and the pig's feet were eaten. The kidneys, liver, heart and head were made into head cheese. Its blood was mixed with flour and baked to make blood bread. We even made soap from the fat.

The meat parts became hams. They were salted in the big salt bins. Some were smoked in a neighbor's smoke sauna--but always in late spring before summertime.

Barsas Gården

THE BEGINNING OF WINTER

The days grew shorter and colder. Soon the first snowflakes hit our nose and eyelashes and warm, woolen mittens had to be put on. Now we wore warm socks and thick coats and hats. We walked to school for two miles in darkness and when we returned home around four o'clock, it was almost dark again.

Christmas

ADVENT

We began the Christmas season by lighting the first candle on our Advent candlestick. This is always done on the first Sunday in December.

There were only four candles to mark the four weeks until Christmas. Every Sunday we lit another candle until Christmas arrived. In Swedish, Christmas is called, *Jultid* (Yul-teed). "Merry Christmas" is "Gud Jul" (Good Yul). By the time we lit the third candle, we were really in the holiday spirit!

LUCIA DAY

On the thirteenth of December, we celebrated Lucia Day. Santa Lucia was a girl who wanted to dedicate her life to helping the poor.

The community celebrates by choosing a teenage girl to represent the Santa Lucia. She dresses up in a long, white gown with a red sash. On her head, she dons a green wreath with white candles. (They use electrical ones now.) Outside, the Lucia wears a little, white, fur coat, as do her four maidens.

She brings cheer to the elderly, the poor and the sick, with songs, small gifts and even large sums of money for destitute families.

In Lovisa, the Lucia with her entourage of maidens, ride around the marketplace on a float that looks like a large, white, shimmering seashell. Traditionally, the buildings around the marketplace have two candles in every window.

Outside is darkness, but the marketplace is lit up by street lamps. The ground glows white from newly fallen snow. Sometimes snowflakes fall gently on the crowd while the Lucia rides around waving to the public. Afterwards, everyone is invited to the Lutheran cathedral for a short Christmas program.

Christmas

MAMA WAS UNBEATABLE!

To Christmas preparations belong the baking and Mama was unbeatable! She baked for days--first rye bread, then sweet and sour bread, yeast breads, sweet cardamom bread and finally cakes and cookies.

I got to help Mama make gingerbread in the shapes of men and women, pigs, stars and hearts. Mama also made wonderful marmalade candy in orange and pear flavors.

Mama did errands in town and often came home with parcels wrapped in colorful, Christmas wrappings. Sometimes I got to go to town to help carry the parcels.

We stopped at Kasten's Meat Market and Forsell's for fruit, coffee and sweets. Both stores were several steps down from the street level. The most wonderful aromas came up from these shops.

We also stopped at Siren's Flower Shop. Mama picked out fragrant, blue and pink hyacinths or little baskets looking like birds' nests made of twigs with red tulip and greenery around. These were for neighbors with whom we exchanged small gifts.

Night Skating in Lovisa

NIGHT SKATING

As an older girl, every Saturday evening, I learned to do jumps and spins with my friends at the ice skating rink in Lovisa.

The ice skating rink in Lovisa was an outdoor arena lit-up at night. A kind gentleman who had a heart for young

people chaperoned the ice skaters in the evening. He made sure we were safe and stayed out of trouble.

Music played over a loud speaker. Snow fell on our faces as we spun and whirled to the music under a blanket of stars. It was all things romantic—especially if a nice boy liked you.

By the side of the rink, sat a little wooden cabin where everyone went to lace-up their boots. In the middle of the cabin stood a pot-bellied stove with a crackling fire. It made everything warm and cozy before you suited up or came in to warm-up, rosy cheeked and exhausted; exhilarated, after hours of skating.

CHRISTMAS IN SCHOOL

In school, we worked on Christmas plays and decorations. Our school Christmas party was always held on an evening before school break. We always dressed up in our best party dresses or suits, often with shiny black lacquer shoes. Our families were invited and we were jumping with excitement before the Christmas party. We sang Christmas songs in small choirs and the oldest students put on a grand Christmas play.

In the Christmas program one year, the beard of one of the three wise men caught on fire from an angel behind him with a candle.

Barsas Gården

Everyone was running around trying to smother the flames. The fire ended up spreading to the main curtain on the stage before we could extinguish it. We were shook-up but all ended well and we were left with a story to tell.

After the Christmas play, a Santa Claus with helpers brought every student a bag of goodies. The name of each student was called and we were given a lovely, white bag decorated with red hearts and green branches. In every bag was a large apple, a big, gingerbread man, two licorice bars and some candy.

All the students danced ring dances until we were totally, roasting hot and exhausted. It was often in a snow flurry and chilling cold that we walked home again in the dark. We were happy though and looked forward to our Christmas break.

Christmas

DECORATING

Now when school was out for the holidays, we cleaned and scrubbed the house again for days. Out came the brightly-colored, striped, carpet runners Mama had woven and that we had scrubbed so clean at the Patuna seashore in the summertime. We decorated the window sills and tables with pretty, white candles in glass candlesticks shaped like stars.

Margareta and I, especially liked to make decorations. We cut out gold stars from shiny paper, made snowflakes of white paper and wove hearts of green and red paper strips to decorate our Christmas tree.

We also cut fine strips of white and light blue, silk paper. Then we brushed bare birch branches with a glue made of

potato flour and water. We dipped the branches in piles of the silk paper strips which made the branches look as if they were covered with shimmering rim frost.

O, CHRISTMAS TREE

It was time for Papa to take Poju and the log sled to the forest to fetch the Christmas trees. Papa had in the summer already picked out the perfect trees for Grandma and Grandpa and us.

Sometimes Papa even found some lingonberry bush branches in the snow which he brought home to Mama. With it, she made a beautiful green wreath with red ribbons and hung it in the doorway between two rooms.

A few days before Christmas we decorated our Christmas tree with our homemade decorations. We used real, little wax candles and small candies, sometimes red apples, gingerbread cookies and lots of silver glitter. Later on we used colorful glass balls.

The sauna had to be heated. We had a good bath and were clean and ready for the Christmas Eve celebrations. In Finland, we celebrate Christmas, and have our special meal and open our presents on Christmas Eve.

TRADITIONAL HOLIDAY SALADS

For weeks, the frozen, dry, cod fish had been soaking in lye. It was cooked so it almost became like jellyfish in softness. We always served it with a white sauce and lots of salt and white pepper. Mama had already prepared several casseroles for Christmas as well, such as rutabaga, carrot and macaroni casseroles.

According to tradition, we had also mixed up a sill fish and vegetable salad. We cut the cooked carrots, potatoes, beets, pickles, and salty sill fish in cubes and served it with a sauce made of whip cream, mustard, salt, pepper and the juice of beets, enough to color the sauce pink.

THE CHRISTMAS STAR

It was finally Christmas Eve morning. I was up early. In the dark morning, I was looking for the Star of Bethlehem. I saw a huge bright star, probably the planet Venus. No one could change my mind that this was not the real Star of Bethlehem.

My sister had convinced me that the big buildings with a factory pipe in the distance from our house was Jerusalem. We children lived with the reality that the world of the Bible was all around us.

Oats for the Little Sparrows

CHRISTMAS FOR THE ANIMALS

Papa gave all the animals an extra portion of hay and oats in honor of Christmas. A sieve of oats, especially stored

from the harvest, was placed in an apple tree outside our kitchen window for the birds.

The birds, pretty red cardinals and yellow sparrows and grey sparrows, were thankful for the oats. In the deep snow and cold weather, it was difficult for small birds to find food.

MAMA'S ACTS OF KINDNESS

It was Mama's tradition to stop by the house of her old milk maid with a basket of delicious food items every Christmas Eve. Sometimes we children helped her deliver that and a Christmas package of coffee and candy and a Christmas magazine to the elderly in our village from The Martha Organization.

Everyone was thankful to be remembered and glad for a little visit by us children. Mama was a board member at The Ulrika Nursing Home. Every year she was invited on the morning of Christmas Eve for a little coffee party with the poor and elderly.

CHRISTMAS EVE CELEBRATION

The Christmas table was set in our dining room with the best china, silverware and long stemmed glasses. We had

Barsas Garden

a large candlestick on the table. The Christmas tree glittered in between two, large, wing-backed chairs by the windows.

Then it was time to take the Christmas ham out of the oven. (We children did not like it very much. There was too much fat on it for us.)

We were so glad when Grandpa, Grandma and Aunt Eva all could celebrate Christmas with us. They always came dressed up so nicely.

Before we got seated, we stood behind our chairs and sang the prayer, "In the name of Jesus we sit down to eat, God bless the food we will receive, bless likewise your precious word to feed our souls. Aaaa-men."

We feasted on all the wonderful Christmas food, even though we children mainly ate cooked potatoes and cold cuts with sweet mustard. We hardly had room for any dessert. The prune cobbler served with whipped cream, and Mama's flaky, butter dough, Christmas star pastries with prune jam, were traditional, Finnish, Christmas desserts.

We listened to Bishop Erik Forsell on the radio who prayed for us all and blessed the citizens of Finland. Mama and Papa were thankful. Everyone in our country who had experienced the fear and poverty and death that

war brings, understood how costly and precious our peacetime was.

While Mama and Papa took care of chores in the dairy barn, we children took care of the kitchen chores. Then we entertained Grandpa, Grandma and Aunt Eva with small ring dances. Then all gathered in the big sal, where Papa read the Christmas story from Luke, chapter two, in the big Bible.

Barsas Gården

Opening Presents On Christmas Eve

THE SANTA CLAUS

We sang some beautiful Christmas songs and all of a sudden, we heard some terrible banging on the door. In comes an old Santa Claus with a bag on his shoulder and a large basketful of presents. He asked us if there were any good children and we all with fear answered, "Ja! (Ya) Yes!"

We felt so sorry for Papa. Almost every year he missed the Santa Claus because he had some chores to do in the stable at just that same time.

After we opened our presents from the Santa Claus, usually we got a newly published book, suitable for each age group, old and young. We got some toys and new clothes, sometimes new skis or a sled or ice skates and sweets in our stockings. We were all thrilled with our Christmas gifts.

One year, the Santa Claus and his wife came in so suddenly, they terrified my sister! She wept in panic. Finally, she was swept up in my Aunt Signe's arms who understood her fear and could calm her down.

MY DEAREST WISH

Another year I had been telling everyone that my very dearest wish for Christmas was to get a doll of my own.

Sometimes I was allowed to play with my sister's doll, but it wasn't the same as having your very own. That year, I did not receive one doll, but three dolls! One doll even wore the same dress as my Aunt Eva.

CHRISTMAS WITH THE COUSINS

On Christmas Day, we just rested and stayed at home with our new presents. The following day we went to visit our Aunt Birgit and Uncle Sigurd and cousins in a taxi all the way through snowcapped forests.

We were welcomed with wonderful food and camaraderie. Cousin Åke (Ah-kay) played the most popular songs on the piano. He knew all kinds of waltzes and tangos. Cousin Gunvor had stacks of Donald Duck magazines and Swedish ladies' magazines. We reveled in them for hours.

Then it was time to be picked up again in the same, shiny, black taxi by Brunn's Otto. We did not own a car and there were no buses running during the Christmas holidays.

The Christmas gatherings continued in the village among neighbors until New Year's, but we children mostly wanted to stay home and read our new books.

Christmas

A LOVE FOR READING

Books were some of our favorite Christmas presents. With all the cold, dark winters, reading was a favorite hobby for almost all Finnish people. (We found out later that Finland had one of the highest literacy rates in the world.)

Mama had given each of us such a love for reading. Sometimes she curled up with us in our beds and read to us. We loved to read Astrid Lindgrid's *Pippi Longstocking* and *Emil* stories, Hans Christian Anderson's funny and sad fairy tales, *Pilgrim's Progress* and Umo Axelsson's missionary stories from the jungles of India.

We were very much affected by the exciting stories of adventure and danger in the jungles of India. People in the jungle were often attacked, killed and eaten by wild animals such as tigers and leopards.

We were horrified by the custom in India that when a husband died, his wife had to die with him…on a float in the water set afire.

We thought the missionaries were so brave, preaching the gospel to the Indian people. The stories showed how God protected them from all kinds of danger.

PRAYERS AT BEDTIME

We trusted God and felt secure that He would keep us if we faithfully remembered to say our evening prayers. We were taught as toddlers to say our prayers before bedtime. I could never fall asleep until I said the *Gud Som Haver Barnen Kär* (Children of Our Heavenly Father) children's prayer, with meaning.

Gud Som Haver

Gud som haver barnen kär (char),
Se till mig som liten är.
Vart jag mig i världen vänder,
Står min lycka i Guds händer.
Lyckan kommer, lyckan går ,
Den Gud älskar, lyckan får.

God who loves the children, dear,
See how little I am here.
Wherever in this world I wander,
Store my luck in your hands.
Luck is easy come, easy go,
With God's love, luck does grow.

Christmas

BASTUBISIN: The Old Man of the Sauna ~ Our Christmas Visitor

Among the many unique adults in my childhood, Bastubisin, or Reuter (Royter) his real name, was the most memorable. He was a little different from the others because, when he was young, he had fallen down in the hold of a large, cargo ship and his brain had gotten slightly damaged.

He travelled around the villages on a bicycle with a little suitcase tied to the back. In the suitcase were small items for sale: combs, razor blades, safety pins, hairpins, etc. It was very orderly. They all had only slightly been used by himself.

After presenting his wares, he humbly asked for some food and a place to sleep. He had special places that received him regularly. Mama and Papa were one of those that always welcomed him.

Reuter often came on a Saturday, when we had our *bastu* sauna day. He liked to take a good bath and then fall asleep in the *bastun* sauna. That's why we children called him *Basubisin*, the Old Man of the Sauna. Mama had his bedding stored in the attic for his visits. When it was too cold to be in the bastun, he slept on the sofa in our kitchen.

Barsas Gården

My mother said that Reuter spoke the most beautiful Swedish she had ever heard. He was able to converse on every topic, and had a great memory for distances and numbers. When Mama served him his meals, we were astonished at how much he could eat--like a whole loaf of bread at one meal!

As children, we studied Reuter carefully. He was tall and lean. His hair was parted in the middle. Gray and wavy, it reached to his shoulders. We thought he looked like Jesus. I don't know if it was his humble, noble demeanor, or the long knife sheathed in his belt that made us look at him with such respect. We grew up with Reuter visiting over the years, and then, one-by-one, we all moved away from home.

Soon another generation took over the Barsas farmstead. My brother, Ingmar, and his wife, Carita, became the new owners. They continued to receive Reuter and even gave him a bed and his own bedroom to sleep in. He then got to see the next generation of Barsas children growing up.

The last time our family saw Reuter was on a Christmas Eve. He came by as usual asking for some food and lodging. My hospitable sister-in-law said, "You are most welcome at our table! Come, share Christmas dinner with us!" It was a very nice thing to do. In Finland, Christmas Eve is like Christmas Day. Mama said, "It will be well with them who care for the poor and needy." In the Bible,

Christmas

it says that when we are hospitable to a stranger, we may be unknowingly entertaining an angel.

Barsas Gården

Barsas Gården in the Wintertime

THANKFUL

We will never forget all the happy memories growing up together on the Barsas Gården Farmstead in Räfsby. Our playing enlarged our imaginations and our chores and farm duties gave us skills, good character and the satisfaction of a job well done. It built up our confidence

and gave us courage to go out into the world and accomplish just about anything we put our minds to.

I thank God for Mama and Papa. Their mentoring, laboring and sacrificial love for us children made us the people we are today. I am also so grateful for my brother Ingmar, sister Margareta and brother Herbert. I love them all very much.

BARSAS GÅRDEN WISHES

Barsas Gården is written as a little 'historic.' My great wish is to see Barsas Gården preserved as a museum. I believe it would enrich the lives of many. Visitors would be able to explore the grounds and experience a bit of the idyllic life we grew up with on this farmstead in southeast Finland.

www.ingramcontent.com/pod-product-compliance
Lightning Source LLC
LaVergne TN
LVHW051602070426
835507LV00021B/2726